D1208162

# The Zoning Dilemma

A Legal Strategy for Urban Change

# The Zoning Dilemma

A Legal Strategy for Urban Change

## Daniel R. Mandelker

Professor of Law
Washington University

Copyright © 1971
BY THE BOBBS-MERRILL COMPANY, INC.
All Rights Reserved

For Jana

*"Too often, we think of the roles of law in our society in static rather than dynamic terms. Law as it is made by our courts, legislatures, and administrative agencies is not an end in itself; it is a means to policy goals, particularly in the allocation of resources. It is a myth . . . that law's only role is that of constraint, of putting on the brakes. Instead, many legal rules and devices are efficient, flexibly adjustable conduits for change and development."*

——*from a memorandum by Professor J.H. Beuscher*

# TABLE OF CONTENTS

# MAPS, TABLES AND FIGURES

# INTRODUCTION

This book grows out of earlier work of mine in which I have
been concerned with the role of planning in urban development,
and especially with the influence of the comprehensive plan on
the urban development process.[1] During 1959 and 1960 I was
in England to carry out a study of English planning, subsequent-
ly published in book form in 1962 under the title, *Green Belts
and Urban Growth: English Town and Country Planning in Action*. In this book I analyzed the administration of English planning controls, especially as they are applied in newly-urbanizing
areas through the English green belt policy.

My interest in English planning was prompted by the fact
that the English had adopted a system of planning administration which is very different from ours. American zoning, at least
in theory, is based on the regulation of land development
through the enactment of local zoning ordinances which allocate land uses by district. In England there is no zoning ordinance. Development is guided by a plan which contains generalized proposals made more specific through local plans adopted
for more restricted planning areas. Planning permission is required from the local authority as a condition to any new development. An application for planning permission is made to the
local authority, which then decides whether permission should
be granted or withheld under the plan. Review of the local
planning decision is carried out by a national ministry.

The English planning system thus differs in significant ways
from what has come to be expected on the American scene.
Development and land use is not preregulated in detail, as it is
in American zoning ordinances. Permission is required from the
local authority, and that permission is given (if it is forthcom-
ing) in an administrative process whose purpose it is to implement directly the proposals in the comprehensive land use plan.

---

[1] I have also looked at these problems in the urban renewal context.
Mandelker, *The Comprehensive Planning Requirement in Urban Renewal*,
116 U. Pa. L. Rev. 16 (1967).

While zoning "in accordance" with a comprehensive plan has been required by statute in most of the United States, a firm planning foundation for the zoning ordinance has been the exception rather than the rule.

For some time it has been clear to most experienced observers that accommodation to development pressures, especially in urbanizing areas, has brought substantial changes in the American system of zoning control. Through one device or another, the American system of zoning is being adapted to an administrative model tending ever closer to its English cousin. Moreover, at least in some sections of the country, these new administrative techniques are being used to implement more directly the proposals of the comprehensive plan. These tendencies are especially obvious in urbanizing areas, where the difficulties of assigning land use locations in advance have led American zoning agencies to a watchful waiting policy. Most of the major land use decisions are deferred to an administrative process which responds to applications from developers as they are presented for approval to the zoning agencies.

I have wanted for some time to find an American jurisdiction in which I could duplicate my English study, exploring in an American context the problem of applying the development proposals of a comprehensive plan through the techniques of the zoning process. As any study of this kind would require the manipulation of a large number of variables, I also wanted to have access to computer assistance in handling and interpreting the data. With these objectives in mind, I took advantage of a visiting year as Professor of Urban Planning and Political Science at the University of Washington in Seattle to carry out the field study of the planning and zoning process which is reported in these pages. Since King County, the county in which Seattle is located, is a fast-growing urbanizing area[2] which had been carrying out its zoning process in direct implementation of its comprehensive plan, it presented an excellent setting for my work. I had, in addition, the resources and experience of the Urban Data Center at the University of Washington. The Center

---

[2] For an earlier account of growth patterns in the Seattle suburbs, see M.R. Wolfe & Associates, Locational Factors Involved in Suburban Land Development (July, 1961) (on file in School of Architecture Library, University of Washington).

had developed a new computer program, System X, which was adaptable to the study I proposed to undertake. Financial assistance for research help and the computer time used in this study was generously provided by the Walter E. Meyer Research Institute of Law.

The objective of my study was really quite straightforward. I had before me a comprehensive plan which articulated a series of development policies, and I proposed to determine to what extent these policies were carried forward in the zoning process by which they were implemented. I hoped, from the study, to develop some fairly simple conclusions about the way in which the comprehensive plan was implemented in the zoning process, but my study results suggested relationships between planning and zoning which were more complicated than I had imagined. I attempt to explore these relationships in more depth than they have been investigated before, concentrating on problems of implementation which have so far been largely neglected, and considering the impact of planning and of zoning controls at their point of contact—the individual, private ownership. To aid my analysis, I provide a modest conceptual model which I find useful in exploring the interaction of the planning and zoning process with land ownership patterns and the land development market.

However, while the enterprise is tempting, I have not moved on from my study to propose in detail a program for a complete reform of the planning and zoning process, even though I would suggest that reform is very badly needed. Any attempt at so major an effort at this point in time must suffer from our failure to examine rigorously the basis of our planning and zoning controls, and the assumptions under which they operate. For example, the American Law Institute has recently proposed a land development code which is supposed to replace existing state legislation for planning and zoning. One criticism of this code is that it is based on doctrinal assumptions which have not been put to the test of the experience we have accumulated over the last 50 years.

That I am not alone in these concerns is made evident by the publication, as this manuscript was being completed, of a book on the history of zoning in America[3] and a symposium on

[3] S.I. Toll, Zoned American (1969).

problems of land development and urbanization in a leading planning journal.[4] Nothing in these two studies substantially alters what I have said here. The exclusionary origins of zoning are made clear in the study of its historical antecedents. Some of the papers in the urbanization symposium do project models of the land development process which are more complicated than mine. But I would suggest that the development process is difficult to fit into any descriptive model with high explanatory value, primarily because the zoning framework in most American communities is so loose that it does not impose a real constraint. Where this is so, we would expect that land development decisions would be influenced by a variety of factors, of which zoning controls are only one.

Deeper and more complicated legal concerns also underlie these pages. For some time I have been interested in the difficult legal issues that arise in the exercise of powers like zoning which do not require the payment of compensation.[5] Here again the English experience is different, as they have attempted to smooth the impact of their planning system by providing some measure of compensation to landowners who are restricted by regulation, and by requiring some repayment of the gains which are enjoyed by landowners who benefit from favorable treatment. We Americans still get along with a planning and zoning system which requires neither compensation nor recoupment, and so it is not surprising that we find that we make payment for our choice of method in other ways. Thus it was that exemption of existing buildings from regulation was one of the prices that New Yorkers paid for their first zoning ordinance. I would suggest, on a larger scale, that accommodation of American planning and zoning policies to the pressures of the marketplace provides another instance in which society pays for the use of uncompensated restrictions. If the zoning system does not bind too tightly, then the burdens of compensation do not appear that great. It may very well be this kind of accom-

---

[4] Symposium, *The Urbanization Game*, 36 J. Am. Institute of Planners 3-58 (1970).

[5] For discussion of these problems in a highway setting see Mandelker, *Planning the Freeway: Interim Controls in Highway Programs*, 1964 Duke L.J. 439; in the housing field, Mandelker, *Housing Codes, Building Demolition and Just Compensation: A Rationale for the Exercise of Public Powers Over Slum Housing*, 67 Mich. L. Rev. 635 (1969).

modation in American planning and zoning practice which creates the ambiguities in the planning process which I discover,
and which lead me to doubt whether American society, at least
in its present frame of mind, is ready or able to make the kinds
of choices that are necessary to the creation of a stronger planning system. Nevertheless, problems of constitutional limitations in zoning and planning law are very intricate, and much of
the detail in analysis which is essential to a full understanding of
the legal issues is sketched only briefly. My aim is to put these
traditional constitutional issues in a broader frame of reference,
which I find more useful than conventional analysis. I do not
mean to simplify the problems that are involved.

Much of what we do in the land use control field also depends on how we view the inheritance of the law of nuisance,
which I have discussed earlier[6] and which I carry forward in
these pages. My own feeling is that the law of nuisance is a rich
source of experience which is essential to our understanding of
land use control and related problems, and which we have only
begun to comprehend.

This book is intended as much for the urban planner, urban
professional, and students of urban planning and urban problems, as it is for the lawyer and the law student. My hope is that
I have succeeded in presenting the legal issues in a manner
which is adequate to the understanding of the reader who is not
versed in the law, although I would expect that a planner, city
manager, or anyone with even the most limited experience in
local government administration would soon find it necessary to
get very well acquainted with the legal problems of zoning control. Nor have I attempted a detailed background discussion of
the nature of planning and of zoning, assuming some familiarity
with this subject on the reader's part. Anyone who wishes more
instruction can now turn to an excellent recent text on urban
planning,[7] or to the discussion of zoning in the Report of the
National Commission on Urban Problems, the Douglas Commission.[8] I might add that I have saved a presentation of how the

---

[6] Mandelker, *The Role of Law in the Planning Process*, 30 Law &
Contemp. Prob. 26 (1965).

[7] Principles and Practice of Urban Planning (W.I. Goodman & E.C.
Freund eds. 1968), especially Part Four and Part Five.

[8] Report of the Nat'l Comm'n on Urban Problems 199-234 (1968).

zoning system functions for Chapter III, preferring first to elaborate my own perspective on the zoning and planning process. The reader who wishes to start with a more detailed account of the zoning function might begin with those pages.

It is difficult to acknowledge adequately all those who contributed to this study. Irving Berteig, assistant director of the King County Planning Department, and Douglas Spaeth of the department staff, spent many hours in consultation with the author and were most cooperative in making available the zoning files, zoning data, and other material which were essential to my work. All of the members of the King County planning department staff were most helpful and cooperative. Mr. Berteig, Professor Henry Hightower of the University of Washington Department of Planning, and Mr. Charles Barb, Assistant Director, University of Washington Urban Data Center, carefully read and offered many helpful criticisms of an earlier draft of Chapter IV. Mr. Barb also guided the author in his use of the computer and was most generous in giving his time. Professor Charles Leven, Director, Washington University Institute of Urban and Regional Studies, read and offered many helpful comments on Chapter II. Mr. Charles Drebes and Mr. John Judd of the Washington University computer center carried out the Chi Square analysis which is reported in Chapter IV. Background on the apartment zoning cases in suburban Washington was provided by Mr. Sanford Wool, Deputy General Counsel, Maryland-National Capital Park and Planning Commission, and by the lawyers who were involved in these cases.

I must also express my indebtedness to other colleagues of mine who were helpful in a less direct way. Professor Arthur Leff of the Yale Law School, and Professor Roger Montgomery of the School of Architecture at the University of California (Berkeley), discussed many of the ideas contained in this book with me and offered many valuable suggestions. I am particularly indebted to Professor Dan Tarlock of the Indiana University School of Law, whose recent studies of land use planning have been extremely helpful, and whose findings and observations prompted many of my own conclusions. I also acknowledge the contribution of Professor Alan Altshuler's study of city planning,[9] a classic in its field, and of Jack Noble's analysis of the

---

[9] A.A. Altshuler, The City Planning Process (1965).

American zoning system, which now appears in the Douglas Commission report. Mr. Norman Williams, Jr., alerted all of us long ago to the challenge to democratic values that is presented by the land use control system. But this list is only partial, for I count friends and associates in my work too numerous to mention.

I would like to express my gratitude to my research assistants at Washington University School of Law, Dennis Wittman, Edward Klinger, and Stuart Showalter, who carried out many detailed assignments, and to Neil Thomas, a student at Wayne State University School of Law, who carefully researched the cases on apartment zoning. Mrs. Albert Koch faithfully typed more than one copy of the manuscript. The maps were prepared by Raoul Suarez, a student in the Washington University School of Architecture. Those maps illustrating various elements of the King County comprehensive plan are adaptations of the maps appearing in the officially-adopted plan and have been simplified for our purposes.

All of us in the planning and zoning field will always remember Jacob H. Beuscher, Professor of Law at the University of Wisconsin who died unexpectedly in the summer of 1967, and who first saw the need to study planning and zoning in action, as it is practiced, and not only in the opinions of appellate courts. His memory lives on in our work.

Daniel R. Mandelker
St. Louis, Missouri
March 15, 1970

# Chapter 1

# LAW AND POLICY IN THE CONTROL
# OF LAND USE

With some confidence it may be said that lawyers were midwives to the birth of urban planning and zoning in this country. Not only were lawyers instrumental in the drafting of the early statutes on which the exercise of the planning and zoning function is based, but lawyers played a major role in the invention of the zoning concept, under which we secured for the first time the comprehensive allocation of land uses in our urban communities. Having fashioned the planning and zoning idea, lawyers took it to the Supreme Court of the United States and won its legal acceptance.

We have now had over half a century of experience with planning and zoning, and the time may well be here to take a close look at what has been accomplished. The urgency of such an inquiry is suggested all the more by current criticisms of planning and zoning, many of which reflect a concern with the larger issues of social equality in our urban environment. We now find, for example, that public housing agencies and builders of subsidized housing meet increasing resistance from neighborhood groups and suburban governments, which seek through zoning to exclude low income housing from their doorsteps. Exclusionary zoning practices of this kind have even led to suggestions that local zoning ordinances be preempted by federal legislation whenever they impede our housing programs. So negative a legal response demands pause. We ought to examine more rigorously the legal postulates on which planning and zoning are based, before we make so drastic a change in the assumptions under which planning and zoning powers are exercised.

This is the inquiry we propose in this book. Our premise is that the conceptual basis for legal intervention in the private market by way of planning and zoning is not only crude, but is not adequate to the demands of an increasingly urban society.

1

We intend to concentrate primarily on the role of the zoning process in the allocation of land for development, and on the influence of the comprehensive plan on the way those zoning allocations are made. To provide concrete examples for our analysis, we will present the results of a field study of planning and zoning practices in the Seattle, Washington, metropolitan area, a fast-growing section of the country where the zoning process was explicitly based on the policies adopted in a countywide comprehensive plan. This chapter begins our inquiry. In it we outline the legal basis for planning and zoning, we consider the problem of judicial review of zoning regulations that implement the comprehensive plan, and we then concentrate on alternative approaches to the legal framework under which the planning and zoning power can be conducted.

## The Legal Framework for Planning and Zoning

Legal techniques for intervening in the control and management of our urban environment fall into two general categories. The law may utilize the power of compulsory land acquisition, known as eminent domain, under which land is taken from its owners subject to payment of compensation for acknowledged public purposes. Urban renewal falls in this category. Alternatively, the law may use the power of regulation, known quaintly to lawyers as the police power, to regulate a variety of activities in the private market for land and housing without payment of compensation to the landowners who are affected. Planning and zoning fall in this category. (We put aside for our analysis, though not to slight their importance, the use of taxing and spending powers and related incentives to accomplish important urban objectives.)

We must now make important legal distinctions between the comprehensive land use plan and the local zoning regulation which implements it. The plan states the development policy for the community, and while it may or may not be adopted by the local legislative body the important point to make legally is that it has no legal effect on its own. The comprehensive plan is made legally effective through local zoning, which covers such matters as building height and site restrictions but which has as its primary function the allocation of land uses throughout the community. Because the zoning ordinance is enacted under what we have called the police power, and so is based on the authority to regulate, it carries important distributive consequences which might startle the casual observer of the American scene. When the use of land is restricted against the wishes of the unconsenting landowner he must bear his losses uncompensated. Conversely, the gains conferred by a favorable zoning regulation go untouched by the community that creates them, for it has no way of recapturing the increase in land value which a favorable zoning creates.[1]

What is more surprising is that responsibility for the conduct of the planning and zoning power rests autonomously at the local level. True, the character of the planning effort has been influenced somewhat by conditions attached to the federal aid that has been available in recent years to assist the conduct of planning activities, but the zoning power is virtually unmarked by federal policy. Nor is the state interest any more pronounced. While zoning and planning must be conducted under and authorized either by a state statute or by a home rule delegation, the statutes are entirely permissive. The content of local policy is not at all determined by the typical state enabling act, which usually does not even mandate the exercise of planning and zoning powers. Exercise of these powers is optional with the municipality, and the content of planning and zoning policy is for local determination. Nor is the situation very different in home rule states.

Autonomy in the exercise of public powers as important as planning and zoning prompts lawyers to ask questions about techniques for their control. We will see later that the plan provides a control over the exercise of the zoning process, since zoning (at least under some statutes) must be in accord with the comprehensive plan. But the plan as well as the zoning regula-

---

[1] Note that throughout these pages we use the word "value" in two senses. At times, as here, we refer to the monetary *value* of land. At other times, we refer to the judgmental *value* preferences which are expressed in the planning process. We trust that the sense in which the word is used will be obvious from its context. For discussion of compensatory techniques which might alleviate some of the problems of monetary loss of value see Mandelker, *Notes from the English: Compensation in Town and Country Planning,* 49 Calif. L. Rev. 699 (1961).

tion is locally adopted, and besides it is the zoning regulation which gives legal content to planning proposals. In England, a national ministry, receiving its mandate directly from Parliament, has a supervisory authority over the planning efforts of local communities. We Americans have no such counterpart. In the absence of any administrative check on the local zoning power from a superior level of government, we have relied historically on the intervention of the courts by way of judicial review to provide a control on the exercise of local regulatory programs such as zoning. Once the zoning process has been completed before the local zoning agencies, the zoning regulation goes unchallenged unless judicial review is brought to bear.

## Judicial Review of the Zoning Process

We have now isolated the zoning process as the legal point of impact at which the public regulation of land use is made legally effective. We might therefore begin our legal analysis of planning and zoning by looking more closely at the zoning power, and since the traditional method of legal control over the local zoning process is by way of judicial review, we might begin with an inquiry into the judicial review function.

We must first make a few comments about the way in which the zoning power is exercised, for both legislative and administrative powers are utilized in the zoning process, and the nature of the power that is used will affect the scope of judicial review. The system is complicated and practically unintelligible, and we will discuss it in more detail later. Here we need only note that the most obvious form of zoning regulation is simply a local ordinance, a legislative act by the governing body which sets up the zoning classifications and then, by way of a zoning map, allocates these classifications throughout the municipality. We concentrate at this point on the nature of this legislative action, and on how the courts handle problems of judicial review when they are asked to question legislative zoning judgments which the local governing body has made. How the courts behave when deciding zoning cases dimensions the judicial response, and sets limits to the influence which court decisions can have on the content of local zoning policy.

We can get a better perspective on the issues that are litigated in zoning by looking first at a program, like the highway program, which relies on the compensatory exercise of powers of public acquisition rather than the noncompensatory regulation of private conduct. To build a highway, property must be "taken" in the physical sense from the private landowner for highway right-of-way and construction. In the highway program, the courts have tended to focus on the compensatory payment to which the affected landowner is entitled under the "just compensation" clause that is found in most constitutions. Of course, some property owners may not be satisfied with the compensatory payment, and may seek to avoid a physical taking by seeking what lawyers call injunctive relief against the highway. Usually, a lawsuit of this kind will ask the court to set aside the route selected for the highway by the state highway agency, on the ground that it is inappropriate and that a better route can be chosen. If the owner is successful in his strategy, his property will have been saved from a taking. But this injunctive power is seldom invoked by the courts. We can fairly say that there is a judicial bias against the use of judicial power to force a halt in program of public improvement based on a compensatory payment which is assumed to do justice to those who are affected.

In zoning, as well, litigants who challenge the zoning ordinance claim that property has unconstitutionally been taken from them. What usually happens is fairly simple. The zoning ordinance calls for one use, the landowner has proposed another, and his land is more valuable on the market for the proposed use than it is for the use that is zoned. Since the zoning restriction carries no compensation, the landowner claims that this restriction on use is an unconstitutional taking of property. The difference in the zoning case is that the landowner is apparently not entitled to ask for compensation from the locality for the restriction that has been imposed on him. [2] Instead, he asks the court for the very injunctive relief which in the highway case it was so reluctant to give. If he is successful, the court will give him an injunction setting aside the zoning

---

[2] See Beuscher, *Some Tentative Notes on the Integration of Police Power and Eminent Domain by the Courts: So-Called Inverse or Reverse Condemnation*, 1968 Urban Law Ann. 1.

ordinance as it affects his property. No mechanism exists in American practice under which the community can then impose the zoning restriction on the landowner subject to the payment of compensation for the loss in value which zoning imposes.

What should be clear immediately is that in the conventional highway taking case, as in the conventional zoning case, the litigant is the property owner immediately affected, and it is up to him to frame the issues which come to the court for attention. We now face a constituency problem. The fact is that the legal issues in both the highway and zoning examples raise problems beyond the perceptions and interests of the litigant immediately affected. Whether the litigant at the bar can or will raise these issues is another matter. In eminent domain cases, for example, important questions in the program which the individual taking supports must often be deferred for challenge until late in the day, usually until some formal step has been taken against the landowner who is subject to condemnation. In zoning cases, the landowner's challenge comes closer to the point of impact, but his own strategy may foreclose an attack on the larger issues.

While the increasing availability of taxpayer's suits may improve the opportunities for judicial intervention in programs like highways in which public expenditure is at stake, in zoning cases there is no taxpayer's interest to assert. The hope for widening judicial inquiry in zoning cases lies with third-party litigants who wish to raise issues that may not be of concern to the landowner immediately affected. We might note at once that even in the face of recent judicial expansion of the role of the third-party litigant in environmental lawsuits, important interests may remain excluded because the courts continue to require some demonstrable link between the action taken and the interest asserted. It may be arguable, for example, whether Negroes living in the city core may assert an interest in challenging racially exclusionary zoning in the suburbs, although the courts' answer to this kind of challenge should not necessarily be assumed. Courts merely enforce an age-old prejudice against advisory opinions in hypothetical litigation when they insist that the interest asserted be real and demonstrable.

For these reasons, when third-party litigants have been recognized they have usually been within some definable range of

impact of the highway taking or the zoning decision. Historically, for example, third-party litigants whose land has not been
physically taken by the highway have been denied compensation when they assert some intangible harm, such as increased
noise, which results from the highway improvement.[3] Modification of this doctrine to allow recovery in these cases has usually
been limited to situations in which some physical or physically-
based damage can be found. In zoning, the courts have insisted
that third-party litigants be restricted to neighboring property
owners who can assert damage to an interest which arises out of
the zoning decision. These problems become more acute in the
case of a zoning action which is favorable rather than unfavorable to the developer. The reason is that in the first case, in
which the zoning is favorable, the *only* challenger is the third-
party neighboring litigant who objects to the landowner's good
fortune.

We will return in later chapters to these problems of justiciable interest in zoning litigation. While not the only perspective
on the formulation of the legal issues, the party-in-interest problem helps us to understand an important limitation on the role
of the courts in zoning, for the courts will be limited to consider what the parties are permitted to present.

## The Judicial Role in Zoning

With this background in mind, we may now take a closer
look at zoning litigation to see what issues might be presented
for consideration by the court. Let us simplify our inquiry by
assuming that the use permitted by the zoning ordinance is a
reasonable one under all the circumstances. That is, the landowner may put his land to the zoned use. The problem is that
he wishes to put his land to a use which is more profitable to
him, but which the zoning ordinance prohibits. Let us assume
that the landowner wishes to build an office building on a plot
which the municipality, unfortunately from his point of view,
has zoned to a single family use. Unless the municipality is a
very small one, chances are that office buildings have been per-

---

[3] *See* Spater, *Noise and the Law*, 63 Mich. L. Rev. 1373 (1965).

mitted elsewhere within its limits. Indeed, the facts are that in this case, which is a real one, the construction of an office building had been permitted by the municipality at a point not very far from our landowner's tract. He asserts that the refusal to allow an office building on his tract makes the zoning ordinance unconstitutional as it is applied to him.

What issues are open to the court for adjudication? There are two possibilities. It might question the criteria under which the distribution of office development has been made throughout the municipality. In this event, it would question the wisdom of the policy judgments which were used to make office development allocations. In the alternative the court might accept the criteria under which office allocations were made, and content itself with an examination of the way in which these criteria have been applied. If the court took the second approach, it would be checking on the consistency with which the municipality's criteria had been implemented. Within the framework of a particular case, the issue is one of fairness. The landowner argues that the zoning ordinance has been applied inequitably, as other owners have been allowed to capture the developmental advantages of office locations while he has been denied the same opportunity. Basic to his contention, of course, is an allegation that the circumstances of the more-favored owners are essentially the same as his. If they are different, and if the differences in location require different results under the policy criteria, then he has no complaint. If these differences do not exist, or if differences exist which cannot be justified before the court, then in conventional constitutional terms he claims a denial of the Equal Protection of the Law.

We will find later that communities do not always articulate clearly the policies under which they make distinctions among competing applicants for zoning allocations. Moreover, the need to justify policy differences in the physical character of the environment in which development takes place has created difficulties for the courts. Here it is only necessary to say that the courts for the most part have refused to inquire either into the basis of policy or its fairness in application, at the same time leaving the door open for judicial intervention when they think it necessary. These tendencies are evident in a pair of cases which perhaps represent extremes of view when we compare the majority opinion in one case with the dissenting opinion in another. Our office developer case is *Robinson v. City of Bloomfield Hills.*[4] This zoning case arose in a suburb on the edge of the Detroit metropolitan area. In an opinion which refused' to examine the policy basis for the zoning decision, either in the broader or narrower sense we have described a-bove, the court strictly limited the scope of judicial inquiry into zoning matters:

> But many of the cases coming to us involve merely the legislative judgment. They are the peripheral problems (should the line be drawn here, or there?) and the allegations of more ad-vantageous use, with its corollary of "confisca-tion" (the property is worth more if devoted to some other use). Save in the most extreme in-stances, involving clearly whimsical action, we will not disturb the legislative judgment.[5]

With this case compare *Vickers v. Township Comm. of Glouces-ter Twp.*[6] In *Vickers,* a developer who wanted to operate a mobile home park was prevented from doing so by an ordinance which had the effect of precluding the development of mobile home parks anywhere in the municipality. Applying the usual presumption of constitutionality, the majority opinion refused to examine the policy basis of the exclusion. With this self denial the dissenting justice was furious. Noting the undesirable social effects of the exclusion, he called for a much broader view of the judicial function:

> Proper judicial review to me can be nothing less than an objective, realistic consideration of the setting—the evils or conditions sought to be rem-edied, a full and comparative appraisal of the public interest involved and the private rights

---

[4] 350 Mich. 425, 86 N.W.2d 166 (1957).

[5] *Id.* at 437, 86 N.W.2d at 172.

[6] 37 N.J. 232, 181 A.2d 129 (1962), *appeal dismissed,* 371 U.S. 233 (1963).

> affected, both from the local and broader as-
> pects, and a thorough weighing of all factors,
> with government entitled to win if the scales are
> at least balanced or even a little less so. Of
> course, such a process involves judgment. . . .
> But that is what judges are for.[7]

Notice that an important dimension of local zoning policy obscures the real issue in these cases. In *Bloomfield Hills*, some office development had been allowed in the community. In *Vickers*, no mobile home parks whatever were to be allowed. Would the majority in *Bloomfield Hills* and the dissenting justice in *Vickers* change places if *no* office development were allowed in *Bloomfield Hills*, but if *some* mobile homes had been allowed in *Vickers*? We submit that they would not. If the opinion writers are serious, then a total exclusion of office buildings would have been just as much precluded from review as a decision to restrict their location to certain areas of the municipality, while the allocation of mobile homes within the municipality would have been just as much subject to judicial scrutiny as the decision to exclude them altogether. Neverthe-less, it is true that the zoning regulation is dimensioned by the municipality that makes it, and that the legal objections to that regulation will differ depending on what regulation is adopted. If some mobile homes are allowed and yours is not, your argu-ment is one of equity, that you have been treated unfairly, and that in legal terms you have been denied the Equal Protection of the Laws. But in this type of Equal Protection controversy in zoning cases the *Bloomfield Hills* case represents the current of judicial authority that refuses to intervene.

When no mobile home allocation has been made within the municipality, then no Equal Protection argument can be made within the regulatory framework of that community. It is just for this reason that the New Jersey court, among others, has in other cases stepped outside municipal boundaries. It evaluates an exclusionary municipal zoning decision on the basis of zon-ing allocations throughout the region in which the challenged

---

[7] *Id.* at 260, 181 A.2d at 144.

municipality is located. These cases thus raise important questions about the locus of regulatory power in the zoning process, to which we will return later. For the most part, however, our attention will focus on allocation decisions within municipalities, and not on the problem of zoning exclusions. When we focus on these internal allocations, we can see that the decisional approach of a case like *Bloomfield Hills* permits avoidance of the important policy-making and value-laden issues. Presumptions of constitutionality allow the court to avoid admitting that it is favoring one land use allocation over another, especially as the presumption is not conclusive and courts do and will intervene to upset local zoning judgments when they consider them erroneous. When they do intervene, moreover, the courts often focus not on the policy implications of the zoning regulation but on aspects of that regulation which superficially do not have a policy content. Thus the court may find that the zoning ordinance has seriously deprived the landowner of the "value" of his property, and so is confiscatory and unconstitutional, or that the zoning allocation in the case under review has not been fairly and equitably made. Generally, however, the courts have left local zoning agencies relatively free of judicial control, and the ad hoc nature of their decisions when they do intervene leaves those affected with very little in the way of guidance for future cases. It is an understandable judicial stance in the face of controversies that involve intense conflicts of interest with a heavy payoff for the winners.

### *Alternative Approaches to the Role of the Legal System in Urban Planning*

This unsatisfactory state of legal affairs has prompted a series of efforts to redefine the role of the legal system in planning and zoning. Some of these efforts have come about through scholarly reappraisal, while in other instances pressures have been brought to bear against the conventional judicial role in land use controversies. Moreover, while the focus to some extent has been on a redefinition of the judicial role in zoning disputes, which we have been considering, in other instances wider issues have been raised, and attention has been directed more expansively to the proper legal basis for the exercise of the comprehensive planning function.

1. *The "taking" approach.* We have already noted that the conventional legal issues that arise in zoning controversies center around the claim by the landowner that restrictions on the use of his land unconstitutionally take property rights from him and so, in legal terms, deprive him of his property without compensation having been paid. Some approaches to a redefinition of the judicial task in reviewing zoning decisions emphasize the problems of applying noncompensatory regulations to nonassenting property owners, and attempt a rationale for the exercise of these powers which can pull together the discordant and conflicting approaches which are obvious to any critical reader of the judicial opinions. Perhaps the most notable of these efforts has been attempted by Professor Joseph Sax, now of the University of Michigan Law School.[8] Sax is skeptical of the conventional analysis we have sketched above, which measures the landowner's constitutional protection by the magnitude of the loss he suffers from the zoning restriction. For one thing, he notes serious definitional problems in applying this analysis. [9] Degree of loss, rather than the absolute magnitude of that loss, would seem to be the critical problem, but the courts have not usually dealt with the issue in those terms.

We would like to add another insight. Neither the zoning restriction nor the developer's different and proposed use have an absolute quality, but derive their significance from the planning and zoning framework of the entire community. For example, let us suppose a comprehensive plan which proposes a very tight developmental framework for the community, with most development concentrated at high intensities at limited points. It is clear, is it not, in those areas of the community not favored by the plan's high intensity development proposals, that the zoning restriction will be comparatively strict? Moreover, if the

---

[8] Sax, *Takings and the Police Power,* 74 Yale L.J. 36 (1964). For other extremely helpful discussions of some of the same problems see Dunham, *A Legal and Economic Basis for City Planning,* 58 Colum. L. Rev. 650 (1958); Michelman, *Property, Utility, and Fairness: Comments on the Ethical Foundations of "Just Compensation" Law,* 80 Harv. L. Rev. 1165 (1967).

[9] Sax, *supra* note 8, at 60.

plan and ordinance do not allocate enough land to meet the demand for intensive development that does exist, then developers foreclosed from these areas will invade the more restricted sectors of the community. When they do, they will be able to allege quite convincingly that the ordinance imposes a loss of considerable magnitude. The question is whether it should be recognized.

Sax recognizes this problem in his statement of the rule that should be applied in determining whether compensation should be payable:[10]

> [W]hen an individual or limited group in society sustains a detriment to legally acquired existing economic values as a consequence of government activity which enhances the economic value of some government enterprise, then the act is a taking, and compensation is constitutionally required; but when the challenged act is an improvement of the public condition through resolution of conflict within the private sector of the society, compensation is not constitutionally required.

We do not wish to pursue in depth the solution which Sax proposes, for we would suggest that the policy-charged character of most public decisions about the physical environment will inhibit any attempt by the judiciary to become systematic in their approaches to constitutional limitations. Our insight is that courts wish to preserve the flexibility of ad hoc intervention in the name of unconstitutionally imposed restrictions to prevent what they see as abuses of power, without specifying the basis for intervening to prevent those abuses. But we are intrigued by the thought that governmental regulation of private interests without compensation—as through zoning—is supportable whenever its aim is the resolution of conflict. The more interesting problem is whether the exercise of planning and of the subordinate zoning power is based only on conflict mediation, or whether it has the more comprehensive responsi-

---

[10] *Id.* at 67.

bility of allocating development opportunities throughout the community in the name of a larger public interest. If the purpose of planning and zoning is to carry out this more comprehensive responsibility, then we ought to examine more closely the basis on which the planning and allocation function might rest.

2. *The planning and allocation process.* Perhaps the most important effort to probe the legal basis of the planning and allocation function is an article by Professor Charles Reich of the Yale Law School on *The Law of the Planned Society.* [11] Reich concentrates largely on the federal regulatory agencies, noting that they have moved "backwards into planning." Originally empowered merely to regulate the industries placed under their charge, they have increasingly become concerned with what Reich calls allocation and planning problems. Thus the Civil Aeronautics Board "unavoidably plans the nation's air transportation system" when it makes individual route awards. Other agencies are explicitly empowered to consider a comprehensive plan for allocation in making individual decisions. We would suggest that in land use control the second mode has been typical, as the individual zoning decision has always been implementary of a comprehensive plan. Nonetheless, Reich's insight that a planning decision is implicit in an implementary decision is useful. Even without an adopted plan for the community, the pattern of zoning decision in that community becomes, in the aggregate, a plan for the allocation of land use. Moreover, land, like air routes and air waves, is a scarce resource. Thus the need to allocate.

Reich then turns to the "central myth" that underlies decision-making in a context in which allocation and planning considerations are paramount.

The myth begins with the assumption that there is an objective reference for the concept of what is best. The process of decision may therefore be carried on in accordance with standards or criteria—that is, within the limits of law.[12]

---

[11] 75 Yale L.J. 1227 (1966).

[12] *Id.* at 1235.

But Reich does not believe that planning and allocation decisions can be made under objective criteria. Instead, he sees "resource allocation as a process by which some are punished and others rewarded for reasons which have no relation to objective merits but have relation only to government policy."[13] In other words, inequalities occur within allocation systems, and Reich questions whether allocation systems can or should preserve equality while carrying out and implementing the aims of government policy.[14] Ultimately, the problem is a choice of values:

> Regulatory law, no matter how radical, proceeds upon the theory that its function is to be a traffic officer. . . . Thus the first zoning laws primarily tried to keep the different uses of land from interfering with each other. . . . Planning begins when the law asks what *should* be; it is here that the ability of planning to choose values becomes a critical issue.[15]

Reich's analysis of zoning fits the Sax concept of government regulation as conflict mediation. Zoning emerged, as Reich suggests, as a regulator of conflicting interests with frictional byproduct effects, and Reich sees planning and allocation as a "compromise among powerful private interests."[16]

In the field of land use control, however, the interests may be private, but they are not always powerful. Moreover, differences in the underlying legal basis for decision-making changes the nature of the planning and allocation function in the area of land use. To some extent, of course, private developers compete for land allocations just as television stations compete for channel allocations. But the difference comes in the concept of private interest that underlies the regulatory system. Governmental interest in the airwaves is plenary, and there is no private interest subject to protection except as accorded by the regulatory

---

[13] *Id.* at 1237.
[14] *Id.* at 1246.
[15] *Id.* at 1247.
[16] *Id.* at 1239.

statute. Access to the airwaves is dependent on the government-al allocation system. But government does not own the land. Ownership, to push legal definitions, is divided, with legal title in the private owner and "ownership" of the use in government to the extent that government regulation affects what may and what may not be done with the property. This division in own-ership, as we see it, is reflected in judicial recognition of the owner's developmental interest in land which is entitled to con-stitutional protection. Public restriction of this interest must be justified, and the justification of this restriction in a constitu-tional setting takes on a different aspect, say, than the plenary regulation of the airwaves or of air routes by a federal regula-tory agency. As Reich suggests, however, we find this justifi-cation in reliance on the general welfare, or "public interest." We will have to ask if the public interest as a basis for decision is as elusive in the land development field as it is in the areas of federal regulation on which Reich concentrates.

   3. *The "new" Equal Protection.* We noted earlier that land use and zoning decisions raise problems of fairness in land use allocations, and we have seen that Professor Reich has general-ized our observations to note that implementation of a planning policy which is value-laden will necessarily create unfairness as some lose and some gain in the application of that policy. We also saw that courts were generally reluctant to intervene in zoning disputes in which the issue was essentially one of fairness in a narrower sense: was the zoning line properly drawn in the case at hand? Recently, however, emerging issues with racial implications have created new difficulties in zoning adminis-tration, and raise a "new" Equal Protection problem with dis-tinctively racial dimensions. Unfairness based solely on land use allocations may not have been justiciable. But unfairness based on land use allocations with a racial component is. Reich may doubt whether society (and the courts) will insist on equity throughout the allocation and planning process, but it is clear that equity and fairness will be required whenever racial issues are paramount.

   We may now note some unique characteristics of the new Equal Protection cases in which racial issues are presented. One is that the litigant does not secure his judicial stance on a "tak-ing" ground. In other words, his standing in court does not arise from the fact that his land has been regulated without compensation to him. Rather, litigants in these cases have been third-party claimants who argue that enforcement of the zoning ordinance has harmed them in ways which require constitutional redress. Note, therefore, that the new Equal Protection cases force judicial recognition of the very interests which were obscured and forgotten in conventional legal doctrine. For example, adjacent third-party property owners may have had standing to object to rezones considered detrimental to them, and developers may have had standing to object to a denial of zoning which limited their development options, but it was difficult to litigate the more general questions of policy which zoning ordinances raised. Thus in our mobile home case the developer saw fit to raise the exclusionary issue. Mobile home dwellers excluded from the community would not have been in this position.

Recognition of a new class of litigant is recognition of a new legal right. Every indication is that harmful practices in zoning policy will increasingly be put to the test in litigation, and that courts will be pressed to accord standing to third-party litigants who raise issues beyond those immediately concerned. Thus, in *Ranjel v. City of Lansing*,[17] Negroes and Mexican-Americans successfully sought standing in a lower federal court to challenge a zoning referendum which if successful would have cancelled a rezoning decision which permitted a Turnkey public housing project in a white neighborhood. Unlike potential mobile home dwellers in our New Jersey case, potential public housing occupants were given standing in *Ranjel* to litigate their right to live in what was previously a closed neighborhood.

What needs to be made clear is that the racial basis of judicial intervention in these cases should not hide the fact that when courts take jurisdiction on racial grounds they necessarily intrude themselves into policy-making questions from which they had previously withdrawn. In our office development case, for example, the Michigan supreme court refused to look at the policy for office location in that Detroit suburb. But the federal court in *Ranjel* was concerned with the city's policy for racial

---

[17] Ranjel v. City of Lansing, 293 F. Supp. 301 (W.D. Mich.), *rev'd*, 417 F.2d 321 (6th Cir. 1969), cert. denied, 90 S. Ct. 1105 (1970).

dispersal of Negroes within its jurisdiction. Lansing's policy was positive rather than negative, but the accident of attitude does not hide the fact that the court did consider the policy basis of the zoning process. Similarly, a federal Court of Appeals in the East reviewed a local urban renewal agency's land disposition policy when passing on the question of equal (and constitutional) treatment of Negroes displaced from an urban renewal project.[18] The court was candid in admitting that a judicially-enforced edict on such policy questions as the scope of the community's public housing effort might be necessary to a successful resolution of the case, although it hung back from taking so radical a step.

Critics may answer that courts in the school segregation cases have for years been imposing policy decisions with a racial component on local school boards, and that the assumption of this authority by courts in zoning and other developmental controversies is in the same tradition and less radical than it would seem. It is also true, however, that intervention on racial grounds in local educational practices has had profound effects on local educational policies. We should not be surprised if we find the same results in the environmental field.

## Conclusion

Let us see how far we have come. The issues are complex, and we have seen that the way in which the questions are formulated has much to do with the legal justification for public intervention in the marketplace of private decisions. One approach to these problems is to start with the equity question which we have been discussing in these pages. We noted that the courts were reluctant to intervene in the name of fairness to upset zoning regulations under traditional objections that they favored one property owner rather than another. But courts could not hang back, we suggested, when the unfairness had racial overtones, and we might expect increasing judicial attention to the problems of racial fairness in zoning cases.[19]

---

[18] Norwalk CORE v. Norwalk Redevelopment Agency, 395 F.2d 920 (2d Cir. 1968).

[19] *See* Sager, *Tight Little Islands: Exclusionary Zoning, Equal Protection, and the Indigent*, 21 Stan. L. Rev. 767 (1969).

Professor Reich does not discuss the racial problem, but he is apparently unwilling to insist on fairness whenever allocative and planning decisions are made in the name of a larger public interest. The problem is, as Reich points out, that the public interest in planning is undefinable except in terms of value preferences unless, as he suggests, the zoning power with which we are concerned can be justified as an "objective" regulation of land use conflict. We can see that Reich's formulation may well be acceptable under some circumstances. Thus a suburban county may determine that different quadrants of an Interstate highway interchange should be developed differently. This policy conveys a model of development which confers inequalities; one quadrant of an interchange may be intensively developed while another may not. The policy implies a choice of values about the distribution of development opportunities at interchanges, but the criteria to implement these policies—an example would be to allow shopping center development in one quadrant only—are objective.

We should now note that a definition or redefinition of role will affect the character of the policies and criteria which are applied in the planning and allocation process. Zoning has not conventionally been used in a positive fashion to implement the straightforward developmental tradeoffs which appear so explicitly in our interchange example. Neither is the more limited role of zoning as a mediator of land use conflict so easily defined. If the mere adjustment of conflict is the guiding principle in zoning, then it is the nature of that conflict which must be examined. If we find that even the mediation of conflict carries implicit value judgments which are the basis for decision-making, then our "objective" criteria will have shaded into policies, and value judgments will pervade the entire zoning process. Under these conditions, the problems of equity and fairness with which Reich deals are not so easily handled either. While judgmental decisions based on value preferences create inequities which the legal system may not be able to modify, equity and fairness in the application of more objective standards is a concern of the legal system. But if all zoning allocations must fall back on value preference then the objective basis for making distinctions of equity and fairness in the application of zoning criteria also disappears.

How do these insights affect our conception of the value deprivation problem, which we saw as the basis of the landowner's more conventional complaint against the zoning restriction? Here we can only suggest that the nature of that complaint may well be affected by the way in which we characterize the zoning and planning process. Restrictions imposed in the name of objective criteria may possibly find a constitutional justification which can support their application without compensation. We may be less likely to take this position when the restriction is based solely on value judgments which form the basis for the planning and zoning choice. Clearly, we need to probe more deeply into the basis for the exercise of the planning and zoning power, and this we propose to do in the chapter that follows.

# Chapter 2

## ZONING AND THE PLANNING PROCESS: A FRAMEWORK FOR INQUIRY

That all is not well with zoning needs little documentation. It was assailed by conservative critics who saw in it a bold-handed attempt to intervene in what had previously been an unregulated private market. Now it is under increasing attack from combatants on a new left, who see in it a covert and sinister effort to manipulate public controls for purposes of racial and economic exclusion. To make matters worse, evidence of downright corruption, the buying and selling of zoning favors, is increasingly common even in our larger municipalities.[20] That politicians would levy a tax on a land value distribution process is not surprising. What is surprising is the failure so far to develop a framework for analysis of the zoning process which can place in perspective the charges and countercharges of rightist, leftist, and social reformer.

In this chapter we will look more closely at the theoretic and legal basis for the exercise of zoning powers. Our emphasis is on the execution of planning policy in the administration of zoning controls. We will ask whether zoning contemplates "mere" regulation, as Professor Reich suggests, or whether there are important policy choices in the zoning process which require a selection of values, in an exercise which Reich calls and which is commonly known as planning.

To provide a frame of reference for our inquiry, we will limit our investigation substantively to a particularly difficult problem in zoning, one which has been troublesome since the inception of the zoning idea—the exclusion of apartments from suburban, single family residential areas. A variety of factors coalesce to make apartment zoning a useful frame of reference

---

[20] *See* Citizens Comm. on Zoning Practices and Procedures: First Report to the Mayor and City Council (Los Angeles, Cal., July 1968).

21

for a discussion of zoning policy, and of the influence on zoning policy of the comprehensive plan. One is that the separation of apartments from single family residential uses was posed as the critical constitutional issue in the landmark zoning case of *Euclid v. Ambler Realty Co.*,[21] so that much of the rationale for zoning policy turns on that distinction. Developments in housing trends also underline the importance of apartment zoning to a total housing strategy. Recent years have seen a substantial shift toward apartment construction in the residential housing mix, and the apartment boom has continued unabated. Largely, it has been a suburban phenomenon.

Demand for suburban apartment sites has also been augmented by the expanded federal subsidies for private housing development made available by national housing legislation. These subsidies need not necessarily be expended on housing in suburban areas, but higher costs, and clearance and relocation difficulties in central urban areas, have focused attention on opportunities for suburban development. While federally-subsidized housing need not take the form of rental units, both economies in development and the explicit subsidies for rental housing in many of the federal programs suggest that much of the housing constructed under their sponsorship will be in apartment development. Add to this demand a comparable need for scattered sites for low-rent, federally-aided public housing, reinforced by new directions in the federal public housing program, and the emerging importance of suburban apartment zoning policy to the national housing effort appears as even more apparent.

Moreover, the issues raised in apartment zoning now acquire a distinctly racial overtone, not only because of the open occupancy provisions of federal, state, and local fair housing legislation, but even more powerfully because of federally-imposed requirements which condition directly the administration of federal subsidies for public and privately-owned housing. As of this writing, for example, federal public housing regulations require determined efforts to locate new projects outside ghetto areas. We also noted in the last chapter that court challenges to racially discriminatory zoning policies open a new constitution-

---

[21] 272 U.S. 365 (1926).

al dimension in zoning litigation. Critical appraisal of the basis for zoning controls is necessary to an understanding of the constitutional challenge.

## The Externalities Problem and the Law of Nuisance

In this chapter we will develop a conceptual framework for our inquiry into the structure and character of zoning. To make a beginning, we must go back to the thoughts and ideas that prompted the drafting of model zoning legislation in the 1920's, on which much of our contemporary zoning legislation is based. When we go back to these ideas, when we inspect the underlying purpose of the original zoning legislation, we find as Reich has suggested that its dominant rationale was the separation of incompatibilities in land use in order to limit and prevent the visitation of externalities arising out of land use interdependencies in an urban setting. Note that we stress the concept of use, for use is the underlying legal concept on which the zoning ordinance is based. Regulation of land uses was to be carried out legislatively. The local governing body was to create zoning districts throughout the municipality which would provide the basis for use allocations, and those uses that were compatible were to be assigned to the same district. In this manner was the development of the community to be ordered.[22]

We must now focus on a characteristic of zoning which both complicates its implementation and, at the same time, states our problem. In the last chapter we noted a division of ownership in land use regulation, taking liberties with the usual way in which ownership is defined in legal thought. That is, ownership of title to the land continues to rest with the private developer, but the public agency, under the zoning ordinance, regulates the use to which the land is to be put. As stated elsewhere, the exercise of the zoning function is predicated on a "gap hypothesis." [23] While the zoning ordinance contains the legislative allocation of

---

[22] For good exposition of the development of the zoning idea see Report of the National Comm'n on Urban Problems, Building the American City 199-208 (1968).

[23] See Montgomery, Improving the Design Process in Urban Renewal, 31 J. Am. Institute of Planners 7 (1965).

land uses on a community scale, the implementation of the development pattern contemplated by the ordinance is left to private initiative. In other words, there is a gap between the adoption of the zoning framework and its execution in the market place. Implementation of the ordinance depends on an appropriate private market response, both at the right place and at the right time.

But why, if we rely on the private market to implement the zoning ordinance, do we need the zoning ordinance in the first place? Cannot the market be trusted to make land use allocations which are appropriate for the community? In the absence of a zoning ordinance, the community land development pattern would be a summation of a series of development decisions made individually by private entrepreneurs, acting to maximize their own opportunity gains and to minimize their own opportunity costs. Why not assume that the sum of these individual development decisions represents a collective public interest which we can legally sanction? The answer lies in whether we perceive the land market as making perfect or imperfect allocations through the pricing system. We might achieve a helpful perspective on this problem by noting, as we have stated, that each entrepreneur in that market need consider only his own opportunity costs and gains. He is not compelled by the private market to consider the externalities which his own development decision may visit on others. For example, a filling station developer at a prime site in a residential neighborhood is not required to take into his calculations the externalities which his station may visit on neighboring residential landowners, who may object to the noise, traffic, and other inconveniences which the filling station may bring. A zoning ordinance based on the separation of land use incompatibilities must therefore intervene to prevent the visitation of externalities which the private market cannot prevent.[24] By making district allocations predicated on land use separations, zoning ordinances correct for the externalities which the private market need not consider.

We must now make explicit one other assumption which is essential to our analysis. Our filling station example assumed

---

[24] This analysis brings us close to the point of view expressed in Dunham, *A Legal and Economic Basis for City Planning*, 58 Colum. L. Rev. 650 (1958).

that neighboring property owners would indeed be affected by an adjacent filling station operation. That is, we assumed that the market in land use and development was characterized by interdependencies and not independencies insofar as we considered the influence of one use on another.[25] If it is accepted that the land use market is characterized by interdependencies as its basic condition, then it must follow that the pricing system alone cannot provide optimality.[26]

We should note next that attention to the harmful character of externalities has tended to obscure another but equally important aspect of the interdependency problem which presents an equally compelling reason for legal attention. Cases arise in which the externalities are helpful and not harmful, in which the land developer seeks to capture the benefit of external economies in situations in which external diseconomies are not present. Let us assume a large regional shopping center, drawing on the trading area created by surrounding residential development, but so sheltered from it that external diseconomies do not occur. On a busy highway leading to the shopping center, a developer now seeks to build a filling station to capture some of the spillover trade which the shopping center attracts. This second situation is sometimes said to pose a betterment problem. Private developers reap increases in land value from the development of others which has been carried on with the blessing and indeed with the necessary permission of public agencies. We will see that the zoning process may claim some success in preventing the creation of externalities harmful to others. It has not been as successful in dealing with the problem of sequential development in which private developers seek to capture the potential for external economies that abound in the environment. We will look at this problem later, but let us first examine more closely the control of externalities that are considered harmful.

The simple fact is that if imperfections exist in the land market that cannot be handled by the pricing system, then

[25] For an empirical study which casts doubt on the interdependency hypothesis see Crecine, Davis & Jackson, *Urban Property Markets: Some Empirical Results and Their Implications for Municipal Zoning*, 10 J. Law & Econ. 79 (1967).

[26] *See* Davis & Whinston, *The Economics of Complex Systems: The Case of Municipal Zoning*, 17 Kyklos 419 (1964).

these imperfections must be corrected unless we are to give up and accept the inequity. We might refer back to our earlier discussion of inequities in allocation systems, and to our comment that the law becomes involved whenever the publicly-based allocation system leads to unfairness or inequity in its application to particular individuals or landowners. Apparently the unregulated private market is perfectly capable of making its own inequitable distribution of gains and losses. The question is whether the legal responsibility to correct and prevent inequities includes a duty to intervene when these inequities occur outside the legal system but would continue to exist in the absence of legal action. We seem to have assumed the duty to intervene, but the impact of zoning regulation on land use externalities is largely corrective. By separating land uses on the basis of incompatibilities, the zoning ordinance acts to prevent these externalities from taking place.

We should now note that economists take quite a different approach to the same problem. Deriving from a mode of thought which is based on the sovereignty of individual preference, economics tend to favor solutions based on indirect influence through the pricing mechanism in preference to direct controls which alter and even cancel individual choices. When he looks at the problem of harmful externalities which are not handled by the land pricing system, the economist's frequent recourse is to suggest a kind of compulsory pricing which will force the cost of the externality back on its creator.[27] This absorption of externality costs is to be achieved by having the landowner who created these costs pay compensation to the landowner who suffered their consequences. Other solutions rely as an alternative on a bargaining process. An intervening and potentially detrimental land use is to be allowed to bargain its way into the environment by paying off those who might suffer from its activities. What the economist avoids is any direct control over the invader which would prohibit his proposed activities, or which would seriously limit their conduct.

The economist's perspective is nonetheless useful to an understanding of what the legal system contributes to the externality problem. When we turn to the tools which the legal sys-

_____
[27] *See* Coase, *The Problem of Social Cost*, 3 J. Law & Econ. 1 (1960).

tem has made available to handle the problem of external damage from private development, we find an ancient remedy designed explicitly to accomplish just what the economists propose as a way of dealing with externality costs. That remedy is a court action based on what lawyers call a nuisance. It was recognized early in the development of the law, of course, that direct invasions of the property of another should be and were made compensable. Problems soon arose, however, which foreshadowed the economist's concern with the externality issue. If I kept animals on my land, and if my servants and shepherds walked without permission on yours to graze and pasture the flock, that was clearly a direct invasion and gave the law not too much difficulty. What if my retinue faithfully kept their charges penned and enclosed? Then there was no direct invasion. But if your dwelling was located next to my pen and pasture, activities on my land might still be offensive though no direct invasion of your property occurred. It was in situations like this, in which there was damage but no direct invasion, that the law fashioned the action in nuisance.[28]

Here enters another complication. Theoretically, the court in a nuisance lawsuit could either award damages to the wronged party or could enter a court order which prohibited, limited, or modified the activities of the offending landowner. To the extent that the court awarded damages, it was compelling a transfer payment which economists have singled out as one possible solution to the externalities problem. But there were limits. Attitudes toward compensable damage which the law is willing to recognize, and tendencies in the law of nuisance, worked to limit the extent to which courts would order compensatory payments in lawsuits against private developers. When the offending nuisance caused damage with a physical basis that was one thing; damages would be awarded. Soot damage from a smoky factory is one example. But the law has generally been reluctant to credit sensibilities, and so the courts were reluctant to recognize a nuisance based on damage which was merely intangible. A shorthand way of expressing this limitation was to say that injury to the aesthetic sense alone was

---

[28] *Cf.* Aldred's Case [1611] 9 Coke R.D.F. 57b.

not enough to justify an action in nuisance.[29] One result of this limitation was that the courts often found no nuisance at all in these situations. When the court did find a nuisance on the basis of externalities without a physical base it usually limited itself to a coercive order and did not award damages.[30]

It may well have been this judicial attitude which led the legal system away from a system of transfer payments and toward the use of the coercive zoning ordinance as the primary method of land use control. This tendency should not lead us, however, to ignore the fact that application of coercive remedies in nuisance litigation can provide a kind of compensation to the injured landowner. The court does this by forcing the offending landowner to internalize his externalities, by making internal changes in his method of operation which remove the offending activity or change its character so that it is no longer damaging to his neighbor.[31] To the extent that these changes require capital outlays from the offending landowner they represent a kind of compensation to the injured landowner, because they remove the source of the complaint. By the same token, the offending landowner who is far-sighted enough to buffer his activities to reduce or eliminate the annoyance to his neighbors has by his foresight perhaps forestalled litigation against him. One example is the industrial developer who purchases enough excess land for his establishment to put sufficient distance between himself and any nonindustrial neighbors.[32] The extra cost of the extra ground is again a kind of compensation to those who might be affected by the nonresidential activity.

Two recent cases illustrate very well these elements of nuisance litigation as it affects land use. *Nicholson v. Connecticut Half-Way House, Inc.*[33] was an action by plaintiffs, resident property owners in Hartford, Connecticut, against the defend-

---

[29] *See* the discussion in Parkersburg Builders Material Co. v. Barrack, 118 W. Va. 608, 191 S.E. 368, *concurring opinion*, 118 W. Va. 608, 192 S.E. 291 (1937).

[30] *See* Barnes v. Hathorn, 54 Me. 124 (1866); 2 Wood, Nuisances § 880 (3d ed. 1893).

[31] *See* Note, *An Economic Analysis of Land Use Conflicts*, 21 Stan. L. Rev. 293 (1969).

[32] *See* G.M. Neutze, The Suburban Apartment Boom 108 (1968).

[33] 153 Conn. 507, 218 A.2d 383 (1966).

ant, who had bought a house in their block for the express purpose of using it as a rehabilitative treatment center for paroled male prisoners. Up to fifteen men were to be housed at any one time, they would have secured or would have been promised outside employment, and they would be under the care of a resident counselor who would provide them an extensive counseling program. Sex offenders, drug addicts, and alcoholics would be excluded. No violation of any zoning ordinance was alleged, and plaintiffs sued to prohibit permanently the use of the residence for its intended purpose.

The court summarized the plaintiff's objections to the proposed use as follows:

> [T]he fears of the plaintiffs that the residents of defendant's halfway house will commit criminal acts in the neighborhood and the finding [by the court below] that the proposed use has had a depreciative effect on land values in this area .... The real objection of the plaintiffs is to the presence in the neighborhood of persons with a demonstrated capacity for criminal activity. [34]

In an opinion which avoided somewhat the principal issue, the court dismissed the judgment of the court below and found for the defendants on the grounds that plaintiffs' fears and apprehension were based on speculation. There was no proof in the case that parolees housed in the halfway house would indeed commit the criminal acts that were feared. Two earlier Connecticut cases had been mentioned by plaintiffs in support of their action. In one, the court had enjoined in advance the operation of a town dump. This case was distinguished because a dump is a "known quantity" whose attributes could be judged in advance. And a footnote indicated that a dump was, indeed, physically offensive. A second case had enjoined in advance the operation of a funeral parlor in a residential district. That case was "clearly distinguishable on its facts."[35] But is this so? Is the custody, preparation, and movement of dead bodies more

---

[34] *Id.* at 511, 218 A.2d at 385, 386.
[35] *Id.* at 512, 218 A.2d at 386.

or less offensive than housing a group of parolees? Why didn't the court in the funeral parlor case wait to see if offensive activities would, in fact, develop? Parenthetically, many courts will enjoin in advance the operation of funeral parlors in residential neighborhoods. The distinction between these cases and the halfway house case is probably a mixture of taste and judicial inexperience. Funeral parlors are a known quantity; the halfway house is not.

Let us now note very carefully that we have isolated a new dimension in nuisance litigation—time. Since the nuisance action is predicated on injury, the notion is strong in the cases that some act or acts must have been done by the alleged wrongdoer to justify the court's intervention. Probably this judicial disposition grew out of the general bias of the courts in equity cases,[36] which generally adopted the not unwise proposition that their potentially severe remedial powers should be used sparingly. But the emphasis on established activity puts a heavy value on priority of occupation, so that nuisance law can with difficulty be used as a vehicle to allocate land uses over a future time span. On the other hand, local legislative bodies might claim as their legitimate function the making of future land use judgments over land not as yet committed to development. Enter the comprehensive plan, and the zoning ordinance!

Equally instructive on the reaches of the law of nuisance is *Patton v. Westwood Country Club Co.*[37] The facts are simple, if not charming. Plaintiff's home was located adjacent to one of the holes on defendant's golf course. Plaintiff complained that golf balls hit by golfers on defendant's course landed on her property. She sought an injunction. In its decision, the court made much of the fact that plaintiff came to the nuisance; she bought her lot and built her house after the golf course was established. But the court went further:

---

[36] A note is in order for readers who are not lawyers. Until recent times judicial function was divided. The "law" side of the court gave damages as compensation for wrong suffered. The "equity" side of the court had jurisdiction of nuisance cases, for it had the authority to provide the kind of positive relief for which the nuisance cases called. Once the equity side of the court took jurisdiction, however, it also found the power to give damages to the injured party when the circumstances warranted.

[37] 18 Ohio App. 2d 137, 247 N.E.2d 761 (1969).

Also, in 1963 Westwood Country Club did attempt to appease plaintiff by changing the sprin-
kling system on the fifteenth fairway, by moving
the fairway farther away from the Patton premi-
ses, and by planting twenty pine trees opposite
plaintiff's lot. The cost of these changes was approximately $2,000.[38]

Here we have the alleged offender internalizing his externalities
by making changes in his method of operation. We are led to
believe that had the golf club not made these changes voluntar-
ily the court might well have ordered it to do so. But note that
the golf club covered a lot of ground. It had the room to make
whatever adaptations were needed under the circumstances. Perhaps, placing the halfway house in the Connecticut case in extensive grounds *might* have placated some of the neighbors'
fears and apprehensions. Given the size of the house and the
site, it was impossible for the defendant in that case even to
take these steps.

## Zoning and the Regulation of Land Use Conflicts

Our two nuisance cases are recently decided, but they give
us the basic clues to the legal constructs that underlie the evolu-
tion of the power to zone, and its validation by the United
States Supreme Court in the now-famous *Euclid* case. Carrying
along a little further some of the thoughts we developed earlier,
we see the function of zoning as a mediator of conflict, and we
see the basis of that conflict in the incompatibilities which arise
out of something we can call land use. Yet an analysis of our
two latter-day nuisance opinions raises real questions concerning the basis for land use distinctions. What was it in the character of defendant's activity in each of our two cases which led to
the complaint, and to the lawsuit? Certainly there was nothing
inherently objectionable in the defendants' land or structures.
In the halfway house we had an innocent residential dwelling.
In the golf course we had an open and no doubt pleasing land-

---

[38] *Id.* at 142, 247 N.E.2d at 764.

scape. Apparently a residence "used" as a halfway house deserves one kind of judicial treatment, while the very same residence "used" as a funeral parlor deserves another. An open and pleasing landscape receives one kind of judicial treatment if it is used as a park for strolls and picnics, and yet another if it is used for golf.

We have now reached an important turning point in our discussion. We were initially willing to concede that the regulation of land use interdependencies, accomplished in part through the ancient nuisance remedy, was based on externally applied objective criteria which did not have a base in value preferences. This assumption must now be questioned. While many land use incompatibilities are a product of physical damage flowing from close proximity, in many cases the conflict is predicated solely on matters of taste and preference rather than on observable physical effect.[39] Regulation of land use separations based on taste must necessarily carry with it the implicit acceptance of value judgments about the ordering of land development. Certainly this is true of residential zoning, in which the conventional separation of single family dwellings from apartments can only be defended by judgmental preference. Zoning strategies based on this preference carry with them an implicit hierarchal model of residential development in which single family development is favored, and in which upward pressures on these more favored uses are assumed to visit harmful externalities which the legal system should control. These assumptions provide the theoretic underpinning for the fountainhead *Euclid* case, and for much of what passes as municipal zoning.

Let us now turn to a closer examination of the *Euclid* opinion. Had the *Euclid* case simply considered the establishment of land use districts in which physically noxious land uses such as offensive industries were excluded from residential areas, the nuisance analogies would have been quite close and the issues would not have given the United States Supreme Court as much trouble as they did. But the ordinance under review in *Euclid* went further. While the land use regulations under attack were a complex, interrelated network of height, bulk, and use restrictions, what presented the most trouble for court adjudication

---

[39] *See* Davis & Whinston, *supra* note 26.

was the creation of an exclusive residential district from which apartments were excluded. In other words, the *Euclid* ordinance gave explicit legal sanction to the hierarchal land use model we have described, which gives a preferred and protected legal position to single family development. Not only did the Supreme Court borrow explicitly from nuisance analogies in upholding the zoning ordinance in that case, but it recognized at least implicitly that zoning distinctions were founded ultimately on taste and value preferences:

> Thus the question whether the power exists to forbid a . . . particular use, like the question whether a particular thing is a nuisance, is to be determined, not by an abstract consideration of the building or of the thing considered apart, but by considering it in connection with the circumstances and the locality. . . . A nuisance may be merely a right thing in the wrong place,—like a pig in the parlor instead of the barnyard.[40]

Moreover, local legislative decisions on the allocation of land uses, and based on these preferential value judgments, were largely cloaked from judicial review by the Supreme Court's adoption of a presumption of constitutionality which is echoed in the more modern zoning decisions:

> If the validity of the legislative classification for zoning purposes be fairly debatable, the legislative judgment must be allowed to control.[41]

Now it should be remembered that the court in *Euclid* did not have before it an application of the zoning ordinance to a specific piece of property, as in our office developer case discussed in the first chapter. Rather, it was concerned in general with the generic basis of land use allocation which the ordinance had adopted. This concern drove the court to consider the reasons why apartments had been separated from single

---

[40] 272 U.S. 365, at 388.
[41] *Id.*

family residential areas. The Connecticut court refused to find a nuisance on the basis of allegedly undesirable activities in a dwelling which was no different from surrounding residences. Indeed, nuisance law had not recognized the differences between single family homes and apartments to the point that it was willing to exclude apartments in single family residential areas.[42] But the Supreme Court in *Euclid* was forced to find enough of a difference to justify legislative separation of apartment and single family uses. This it did in an enlightening paragraph, which in its explicit consideration of land use dynamics belied the Court's reliance on constitutional presumptions:

> With particular reference to apartment houses, it is pointed out that the development of detached house sections is greatly retarded by the coming of apartment houses, which has sometimes resulted in destroying the entire section for private house purposes; that in such sections very often the apartment house is a mere parasite, constructed in order to take advantage of the open spaces and attractive surroundings created by the residential character of the district. Moreover, the coming of one apartment house is followed by others, interfering by their height and bulk with the free circulation of air and monopolizing the rays of the sun which otherwise would fall upon the smaller homes, and bringing, as their necessary accompaniments, the disturbing noises incident to increased traffic and business, and the occupation, by means of moving and parked automobiles, of larger portions of the streets, thus detracting from their safety and depriving children of the privilege of quiet and open spaces for play, enjoyed by those in more favored localities—until, finally, the residential character of the neighborhood and its

---

[42] A careful search failed to produce any cases of this kind. Cases in which an apartment house is used for illegal purposes, such as prostitution, should be distinguished. State *ex rel.* Brucker v. Robinson, 250 Mich. 99, 229 N.W. 403 (1930).

desirability as a place of detached residences are utterly destroyed. Under these circumstances, apartment houses, which in a different environment would be not only entirely unobjectionable but highly desirable, come very near to being nuisances.[43]

This paragraph carries important implications beyond its simplified model of urban development, and the social attitudes toward urban living which it explicitly incorporates. (This same paragraph, incidentally, was quoted in full in a Michigan Supreme Court opinion decided in 1968!) One important point is that the Supreme Court obviously worked from assumptions about the character of residential development as it existed at the time of the opinion. Note the assumption, for example, that parking would be off-site and not on-site. But the paragraph just quoted leads us to ask which variable in the difference between apartment and single family residences formed the basis for the court's classification and concern? For example, if single family dwellings were built at the same *density* as apartments, wouldn't the parking problems be the same? And if apartments were built at the same *height* as single family dwellings, wouldn't the light and air objections disappear? If we are concerned with a problem of building bulk in relation to site, then it is clear that multiple occupancy units may require some adjustments in site and project design that are not required by single family dwellings. But these adjustments would seem to require adaptation rather than exclusion.

More difficult problems are created by the comparative increase in density which apartment development may bring, and these were not even considered by the *Euclid* opinion. More concentrated residential populations obviously require different kinds of community infrastructure than do more dispersed residential populations, whether we are talking about roads, schools, or the more essential urban services. Density control, moreover, has important consequences for the shape, form, and character of the area which is subject to zoning regulation. But if land use allocations have important consequences for the de-

---

[43] 272 U.S. 365, at 394, 395.

velopmental framework of an urban area, we are led to a broader consideration of what form that framework might take.

We turn next to a consideration of this problem. But we
might conclude our discussion of *Euclid* by noting that it may
well have been the social implications of apartment living that
worried the United States Supreme Court. Isn't that implica-
tion clear from the paragraph last quoted? In a situation in
which it was densities and site planning that obviously created
the externalities, the Court did what the halfway house case
much later refused to do. It generalized the living arrangements
which then typified apartment development into a legally significant "use" category, which then became subject to independ-
ent and less favorable treatment under the umbrella of land use
regulation.


### The Space Component in Land Use Regulation


What if the court in the *Euclid* case had chosen to recognize
the opportunities for internalizing externalities which a very
different kind of apartment development might have provided?
After all, the court in the golf club case was willing to find that
steps taken by the club to cut down on the possibility of stray
golf balls had removed the externalities in that situation. Presumably, apartment developments on larger tracts could handle
the parking and other objections to which the *Euclid* opinion
gave voice. The difficulty, of course, is that apartment development of this kind was simply not known, or was in its infancy,
when the *Euclid* opinion was written.

Nevertheless, from what we have said so far we can see that
the value choices that were implicit in the *Euclid* opinion were
very much affected by the way in which the court handled the
spatial frame of reference within which the zoning allocation
was judged. We might now explore more closely the impact that
the spatial referent for the zoning and planning process has on
the values which are maximized by that process. There are several facets to this concern. One has to do with the character of
the area in which nuisance and zoning law is applied. Since
nuisance law is predicated on a land use hierarchy in which the
single family residential use is accorded the highest status, it

would follow that nuisance law would work best in established residential areas that are fully or substantially developed. We might also expect that nuisance law would not work as well, if at all, in undeveloped areas in which the development pattern was not yet fixed. Indeed, this has been the experience in the nuisance cases. A Connecticut court, in an opinion in which it refused to enjoin the operation of a quarry in an undeveloped area, suggested that it could not provide through court decree the power and authority which is only available through a zoning ordinance.[44] This judicial attitude toward the role of nuisance lawsuits in developing areas highlights the conservative role of nuisance litigation, if by conservative we mean that the nuisance lawsuit was generally used to support land use patterns already established by private initiative and private development.

In developed areas, on the other hand, the zoning ordinance is restricted by the assumption, which received constitutional sanction, that the zoning ordinance may not be applied retroactively to development already in place that is nonconforming to the zoning ordinance at the time of its adoption. It is in developing and urbanizing areas, then, that publicly-adopted land use controls have the greatest role to play. Unfortunately, the antecedents of zoning controls in nuisance law blunt the impact of zoning in those very areas where it can be most useful, for when the development pattern is not yet established the courts may be unwilling to support zoning regulations which impose a zoning pattern.[45] Moreover, there is empiric evidence of reluctance to adopt zoning controls until development is substantially well along and zoning options substantially foreclosed.

Even when nuisance cases arise in areas which are already developed, problems occur in determining the geographic area within which the problem of externalities is to be resolved. This spatial issue is often hidden and inexplicit in the nuisance cases, as in our halfway house case, in which the court must have made the assumption that it was testing the impact of the proposed use only on those neighbors living in the immediate area.

---

[44] Connecticut Bank & Trust Co. v. Mularcik, 22 Conn. Super. 415, 174 A.2d 128 (1961).

[45] The classic case is Arverne Bay Constr. Co. v. Thatcher, 278 N.Y. 222, 15 N.E.2d 587 (1938).

Even when the spatial issue has been made explicit, and the courts have considered and defined the area which is affected by the nuisance, they have often taken a very limited viewpoint. Thus some of the funeral parlor cases have emphasized that the funeral parlor is not a nuisance unless it can be seen![46] Conversely, even satisfying those who are directly affected by the offending use leaves unresolved the impact of the use on those who are more remote physically but who are still affected. [47] We may note, therefore, how the problem of injury in nuisance cases is closely linked to the question of who has standing to raise the issues in zoning cases, which we discussed in our last chapter.

This narrow conception of the spatial framework within which nuisance impacts are examined is in part a consequence of the judicial attitude toward its power to intervene in nuisance cases. Since the courts usually agreed to intervene only when the development pattern was established, they would necessarily be limited to an urban setting in which ownerships had been fragmented and distributed. In the typical single family residential area, each ownership is in a different family, and in the older areas of our urban centers the higher densities will mean that each ownership is relatively small. This development pattern probably led the United States Supreme Court in *Euclid* to take the individual lot as the critical area of legal control, and to consider the problem of external spillovers on that basis. We might note, moreover, that if the court in a nuisance case had widened its point of view it would have involved itself in the policy-making function of land use allocation within the entire community. Nuisance cases attempted to avoid this problem by taking the development pattern of the neighborhood as given. In the zoning cases, the courts reached the same result by refusing to investigate the criteria under which land use allocations were distributed communitywide, as in our office developer case in the last chapter. *Euclid* merely held, as we translate it,

---

[46] *See* Dawson v. Laufersweiler, 241 Iowa 850, 43 N.W.2d 726 (1950).

[47] For discussion of this problem in a standing to sue context see Comment, *Increased Traffic as Meeting the Special Damages Requirement for Aggrieved Party Standing*, 1969 Urban Law Ann. 169.

that land use incompatibilities based on taste could be the or-
ganizing concepts on which these criteria could be formulated.

We have reached a point at which we can begin to formulate
a role for the zoning ordinance and the comprehensive plan
which requires more than the regulation of externalities from a
neighborhood perspective. Our discussion has suggested a basis
for such a role, for it has indicated that selecting the area which
is the spatial referent for planning and zoning policy is critical
to a definition of its function. The point has been excellently
put by Professor Kuhn in another context:

> Thus, in order to distinguish between external
> and internal values it is necessary to pinpoint the
> exact locus of decision-making power. . . . If the
> planning horizon is limited, if the locus of re-
> sponsibility is set low, then few values will be
> internal and many values will be external. As the
> analytical horizon widens . . . an increasing por-
> tion of costs and gains moves into the internal
> sphere. Once his terms of reference are deter-
> mined, the decision maker tends to be guided by
> internal effects only. This really follows defini-
> tionally.[48]

This insight provides us with a valuable analytic tool, for it
explains why a court would consider it important that a golf
course could internalize its externalities by planting a buffer of
trees.

But Professor Kuhn's analysis has application beyond the
level of a specific case. By taking the individual lot as the "locus
of responsibility," we saw a role for the community in the
adjustment of conflict among incompatible land uses. This function gave the community a comparatively passive role in the
setting of development objectives. But the emphasis in role
shifts when we move explicitly to the community rather than
the individual lot as the "locus of responsibility." Spillovers
which are external to the individual lot become internal to the

---

[48] T.E. Kuhn, Public Enterprise Economics and Transport Problems 8
(1962).

community when it calculates the gains and losses of its development policies, and out of this calculus emerges a more positive community contribution. True, even at the community level a community might consider the impact of its planning policy only to the extent that it affects harmful land use interactions. But we have already noted that land use externalities may be positive as well as negative. Not only may the community deal with negative land use externalities, but it may allocate development opportunities based on the capture of positive externalities as well. Within the community, some property owners will be gainers, while some will be losers. But this distribution of development opportunity is justified by the tradeoffs in land use allocation that have occurred at the community level.

As plausible as this extension of the community's role in planning and zoning policy may appear, it obviously raises some difficult questions. Since we have been focusing on judicial reactions to land use controls, we might first ask how the courts might react to a community policy which is positively based on the allocation of development opportunities. Nuisance law arose out of a familiar legal context in which the law merely intervened to give reparation for harm done, so that a zoning power based on the same concept had sound legal antecedents. But judicial acceptance of local allocation of development opportunity not based on harm prevention would require judicial sanction of the extension of the planning and zoning power into unfamiliar territory. For in this situation the planning and zoning choice clearly prefers one site over another solely for reasons of local policy. The decision cannot be referred to a more objective legal standard.

Foreclosing private capture of external economies was indeed the issue, however, in the recent New Jersey case of *Forte v. Borough of Tenafly.* [49] Here a suburban municipality faced the familiar problem of a declining and decaying central business district. Yet commercial development was occurring elsewhere in the municipality. To help preserve and enhance the economic position of the central business district, the municipality amended its zoning ordinance to prevent any major commercial development except in the central commercial core. A

---

[49] 106 N.J. Super. 346, 255 A.2d 804 (App. Div. 1969).

challenge to the ordinance was brought by a developer who wanted to build a supermarket along a busy street which was already highly developed commercially. In other words, he wanted to capture the external economies which were presented by the proximity of similar commercial development elsewhere in the area. Judicial acceptance of the developer's position would have been expected, but in this case the court took the contrary position. It was willing to credit the municipality's decision to protect its downtown core, and on this basis it upheld the constitutionality of the ordinance.

The New Jersey case highlights the role of a positively oriented planning policy in the allocation of development opportunities. (We put aside the protectionist aspects of the case, which are more troublesome.) But the case opens another dimension to the spatial aspect of planning, and to the influence of space on planning values and planning policy. We stated earlier that the selection of the area within which the planning and zoning decision is made is critical to its definition and character. We saw that planning and zoning took on an entirely different character when it dropped the unit of legal ownership—the lot—as the basis of planning and of zoning control, and moved to the community level as the area of concern within which the exercise of planning and zoning powers was to be justified. But the New Jersey case makes it plain that if the community is to accept the responsibility for allocating positive development opportunities within its boundaries, then it must adopt a policy under which those opportunities can be distributed. And this policy will require, as in the New Jersey example, that limits be placed on those areas in which development will be allowed. Those limits may be wide or narrow, but a decision on limits must be made, and it will have important consequences for the planning and zoning system.

Growth is at a premium in our culture, and so we have not faced these problems. Indeed, it can be argued that an unspoken premise of American planning policy is that no barriers should be placed in the way of indefinite urban expansion. The English take a different point of view, and their Green Belt policy is implemented for the very purpose of setting limits to the growth of urban areas. In an American context, Professor Leven has justified the English concern. He has pointed out that setting an edge to the limits of urbanization is perhaps the most important decision that has to be made in an urban development policy.[50] Absent widespread American concern for this issue, at least in local planning practice, let us see what the effect of an urban limits policy on planning and zoning controls might be.

We have illustrated the impact of an urban limits policy in Map 1. The map indicates, schematically, the effect of urban limits on a hypothetical American urban area of moderate size. What is essential to note first is that limiting the edge of urbanization restricts the supply of land relative to demand, with several important consequences for planning and zoning. To simplify our example, we have assumed a planning policy for apartment development which limits potential sites to the quadrants of Interstate freeway interchanges. These are noted diagrammatically on the map. In addition, we will assume that some but not all of the interchange quadrants are to be committed to apartments when the zoning decision is finally made, partly because it is proposed that the other quadrants will carry commercial and other related land uses.

Note the simple fact that accepting the wider rather than the narrower edge as the limit of expansion triples the number of potential sites available for apartments. If we assume that the narrower rather than the wider edge is adopted as the basis for the planning program, the impact on land development will be considerable. Competition among developers for the potential sites will be more intense, as their number is more limited. More competition for fewer sites will inflate prices, increase densities, or both, assuming that the reduction in urban limits is not a response to a decline in demand. Both the character and intensity of development will be affected as keener competition produces more intensive utilization of the available land.

We should also note some important consequences for zoning of the narrow limits policy. Within the wider urban limit, each zoning decision on apartment development restricts the number of sites for additional apartment zones, but the greater availability of sites enhances the possibility that more apart-

---

[50] C.L. Leven, Determinants of the Size and Spatial Form of Urban Areas (Washington University Institute for Urban and Regional Studies, Working Paper SSF 1, March 1969).

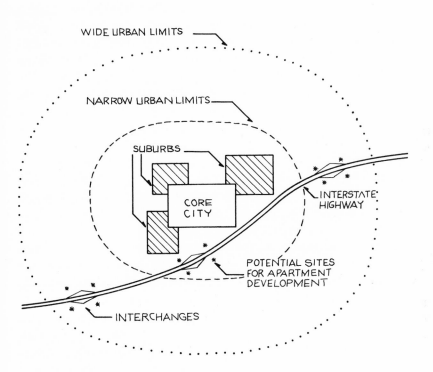

MAP I: IMPACT OF AN URBAN LIMITS POLICY.

ment zoning will be granted. Assuming that the number of zoning sites selected in the wider urban limits policy is more than
will be needed for apartment development in the foreseeable
future, we might even expect that some apartment zoning will
be held back for future use after the zoning has been granted.
Under the narrower policy, the likelihood that development will
follow closely on the zoning is greater, assuming that the number of sites allowed corresponds roughly with demand. Moreover, each zoning decision has greater consequences for community planning policy under the narrow limits approach, because
the comparative scarcity of sites makes each decision on each
site more important to the total planning objective. That is,
each zoning decision narrows substantially the zoning options
which remain open to the municipality.

We have noted earlier that American practice favors wide
limits rather than narrow. We can only speculate why this is so,
but we would suspect that it reflects the need to accommodate
the demand for development opportunities that arises from the
private sector. Adherence to a more constricted policy on urban
growth would require restrictive zoning choices to which the
private market would object, creating pressures which the legal
system would find difficult to withstand. It is for this reason
that green belt or low intensity zoning over wide areas has had
legal difficulty when it has faced the courts.[51]

What we need especially to note is that selection of the
geographic area within which the planning function is to be
conducted has defined the arena in which development opportunities are to be allocated, and externalities limited, by the
planning and zoning process. Within narrow urban limits, for
example, the nature of these allocations and their impact on
their surroundings is different just because, given the area open
to development, the number of sites is fewer. We need only
repeat Kuhn's injunction that a value which is external to the
individual developer becomes a value which is internal to the
community as it pursues its zoning and planning policy within
its spatial frame of reference.

---

[51] Board of County Supervisors v. Carper, 200 Va. 653, 107 S.E.2d
390 (1959). *But see* Norbeck Village Joint Venture v. Montgomery County Council, 254 Md. 59, 254 A.2d 700 (1969).

The importance of this insight to an understanding of the planning and zoning function has influenced our choice of subject in this study. Apartment zoning in suburbia is not only important on its own merits. It provides an opportunity to explore development allocations in a spatial framework in which a decision on urban limits is essential. In more conventional terms, we focus here on regional and countywide planning policies which speak to the problems of land development over wide urbanizing areas.

### The Time Problem in Land Use Regulation

We have already noted that nuisance lawsuits were most effective in areas that had already developed, while the zoning ordinance is arguably most effective in its application to developing areas. This distinction is carried forward in the assumption that court orders in nuisance cases may eliminate uses already in being, while the zoning ordinance may not operate retroactively and is confined to a prospective application. Zoning can do little, therefore, with the problems of fully developed areas, except to hold the line. Its bite comes most as a method of regulating land use allocations in areas as yet unurbanized, or still developing. It is primarily a mechanism for allocating land uses over time in an urbanizing land market.

With this observation in mind, let us look more closely at the timing problem in zoning. We would have expected that much attention would have been paid to the role of the zoning ordinance in regulating the movement of land from nonurban to urban uses, and that the timing of this process would get critical analytic attention. Going back to our urban limits map, for example, we would expect that neither policy would work well if zoning decisions were not followed within a reasonable period by the development which they permitted. Under our narrow limits policy, for example, if all the land to be committed to apartments is zoned, and is then held off the market for some time, the community plan will be seriously frustrated, to say the least. As the initiative for development always lies in the private sector, any system of control such as zoning must begin with a very firm idea of how the private market in land and land development functions. Most important, since the public regulatory system can control the timing of the zoning decision but not the timing of the private response to that decision, we would have expected that zoning would take careful account of the time horizon on which the private market operates.

Unfortunately, we have very little empiric foundation on which to construct a descriptive model of the land market which can give us this information.[52] Moreover, what evidence we do have suggests that the law has made some very simplified and erroneous assumptions about that market. We might first examine the importance of the timing problem to our analysis by returning to our discussion of the constitutional issues in zoning control. Remember our earlier observation that the law's conventional approach to constitutional limitations on the zoning power is to concentrate on the restrictive effect of a zoning ordinance on the would-be developer. That is, the law has conventionally tested for the constitutional limits of zoning by asking whether the restriction on development which the zoning ordinance imposes is an unconstitutional "taking" of property from the landowner. In making its decision on the constitutional issue, the law concentrates on the land itself, and on the development value which is thought to be inherent in the land. It is not that the law will automatically credit as a constitutionally protected interest the increase in development value which the developer claims. Statements are legion in the cases that the difference between the zoned value and the development value is a factor to be considered, but is not controlling on the court. Nevertheless, the law begins with this difference in value as the starting point for judicial inquiry.

---

[52] For a recent investigation of land market problems in urbanizing areas see G. Milgram, The City Expands (March 1967), summarized in Adams, Milgram, Green & Mansfield, *Undeveloped Land Prices During Urbanization: A Micro-Empirical Study over Time*, 50 Rev. Econ. & Statistics 248 (1968). *See also* A.A. Schmid, Converting Land from Rural to Urban Uses (1968). Some of the work on suburban development that has been carried out at the University of North Carolina planning department is summarized in Kaiser, *Locational Decision Factors in a Producer Model of Residential Development*, 44 Land Econ. 351 (1968), and in Kaiser & Weiss, *Decision Agent Models of the Residential Development Process—A Review of Recent Research*, 23 Traffic Q. 597 (1969). *See also* Clawson, *Urban Sprawl and Speculation in Suburban Land*, 38 Land Econ. 99 (1962); Harvey & Clark, *The Nature and Economics of Urban Sprawl*, 41 Land Econ. 1 (1965).

The fact is that this legal approach to constitutional issues simply ignores the way in which the land market functions, and we might now build a very simple descriptive model of our own which provides a more realistic starting point for analysis of the legal questions. Urbanization of raw land requires not only a change in use, but a change in ownership, and a series of changes in ownership at that. Development for urban purposes is not normally carried out by the owner of the land in its raw and undeveloped state. In many cases, of course, there is a purchase by the developer who intends to carry out the development for which a change in zoning is requested. Options to buy, subject to a favorable rezoning, are common. But even if the prospective developer is the real party in interest in the zone change, he may not proceed to development immediately but may hold the rezoned land against his future building needs. In this case he is performing a holding function. Land is being held off the market for urban uses against the contingency that it will be needed for development in the future.

In other instances there will be an intermediary owner of the land who does not have development in mind at all, and whose only entrepreneurial interest is in the capital appreciation of the land for its potential urban uses. This entrepreneur may or may not seek a rezoning of the land consequent upon his purchase. Whether or not he does will probably depend on his own willingness and ability to tolerate the risk that he may or may not be able to get a zoning for an urban and more intensive use at some point in the future. There may also be other buyers and landholders who are intermediary between this first sale of the land and its final development. But the point to make is that whoever performs this holding function has before him as economic incentive the potential of capital gain accruing from an increase in land value arising out of the shift in land use. Some if not the major part of this increase in value is a product of the zoning decision which authorizes the conversion.

The entrepreneur who specializes in acquiring and holding land for potential capital gain is often called a speculator. Whether his influence on the market is baneful or beneficial has been examined elsewhere and will not be explored here.[53] For

---

[53] G.M. Neutze, *supra* note 32, at ch. 6.

purposes of this discussion we will remain neutral on the subject. The important and critical point to make is that the relationship between the zoning decision and the capital gain potential introduces a central element in the land entrepreneur's investment decision.

The point is that the land entrepreneur is willing to forego the certainty of present gain for the possibility of greater gain later. "If the *present value* of the flow of returns from land which is unused for ten years and then used for apartments exceeds that which would result if it were used for single-family houses now, it is in the community interest that it should be held vacant. . . ." (Emphasis supplied)[54] And it is just in this situation that it pays the land entrepreneur from an investment point of view to withhold land from present development in the expectation of future gains. But note the emphasis on *present value* in the quotation. The simple point is that income realized now is more valuable to the investor than income to be realized in the future, because the enjoyment of future income is postponed. It is just for this reason that banks pay interest to depositors. But to arrive at a proper value on the capital gain to be expected in the future we must apply a discount rate to the amount of the expected future gain. Tying up funds in land deprives the investor of other economic opportunities on which he might have enjoyed an immediate rate of return. We must apply that rate to discount, or decrease, the present value of the future gain which the developer expects to realize on his property.

It should immediately be apparent that willingness to postpone a capital gain on land investment is to a large extent a function of the certainty with which that capital gain can be expected to occur. Let us assume a zoning policy under which all land to be used for apartments is zoned in advance by the municipality, and no land to be used for apartments is zoned at the request of a potential developer. In this situation, the certainty that development will take place on the zoned parcels is extremely high, and the future capital gain *except to present owners at the time of the rezone* relatively low. In addition, should the community underzone for potential apartment de-

---

[54] *Id.* at 108.

mand, we would not only expect the value of the prezoned sites to rise rather quickly to their zoned use, but we would also expect the owners of this prezoned land, armed with a favorable zoning, to be prepared to wait out a buyer at the right price. In other words, the certainty of gain would substantially strengthen their holding power.

In fact, the evidence suggests that prezoning for apartment uses rarely occurs on so intensive a scale, and that developers must seek apartment rezones as and when the rezoning is needed. We will explore in a later chapter the impact of a county zoning policy which is based largely on just such a strategy. But the point to make here is that with an increase in uncertainty over zoning decisions for apartment uses, the investment behavior of land entrepreneurs in the land market is quite drastically affected. For example, we might expect under conditions of great uncertainty that present owners would be more willing to sell to land entrepreneurs who intend to hold in anticipation of future gains. But the risks of greater uncertainty will have other effects. In addition to discounting for the normal delay in receiving his anticipated gain, the land entrepreneur must discount for uncertainty as well. That is, he must raise his rate of return to take account of the possibility that he will receive no gain whatsoever. Put it another way. In a zoning system in which the zoning decision is highly uncertain, the land entrepreneur will lose on some parcels and gain on others. He must recoup his losses with his gains if he expects to remain in business. We could spin out endless speculations on the effect of zoning policies with a high uncertainty content. For example, we would expect that one result of zoning uncertainty would be a high level of land banking by developers and entrepreneurs who have the capital base to sustain such practices. That is, we would expect developers and entrepreneurs to acquire land with development potential, holding the land against the possibility of gain arising from general increases in price levels.

We can now return to the constitutional interest of the landowner in zoning regulation. We noted earlier that his constitutional claim relates to the loss of development value which the zoning ordinance forces on him. But this claim is not supportable in the sense in which it is made. It assumes that the law is forcing a deprivation of development value which the owner of the land was entitled to expect. This is hardly the case. In fact, the true party in interest in zoning litigation is the party who is gambling—speculating is another word—on the change of use. To speak of deprivation of expectation in this context is unrealistic.

We might also look more closely at the impact of land holding practices and the operation of the land market on the ability of the zoning system to control development sequence. The problem arises out of the developer's need to know with some degree of certainty where the zoning agencies will allow development to occur. His concern is with his whole universe, with the entire area in which land development is possible. He wants to know at what points in the environment the zoning agency will permit land development at an urban scale. Will apartments be permitted north of the Bothell Freeway or will they be confined to a line south of that point? What is the zoning agency's policy on future apartment development in the Highline area? These general strategies on development will affect his land investment decisions, and his willingness to buy and hold land for future development. Presumably, it is with these aspects of a community development strategy that the zoning and planning agencies should concern themselves when they address planning and zoning policy on a community scale. This was the point in our discussion of the urban limits problem, which we attempted to make concrete in our example of the wide and narrow urban edge. As the limits of urbanization widen the number of potential development sites will increase, and the zoning agencies will find it even more difficult to deal with holdout practices.

To better understand the impact of the holdout problem, let us assume that the comprehensive plan has proposed apartment development in the vicinity of the Northgate shopping center. Now let us assume that a developer secures a substantial apartment zoning in this area, but then withholds development in the expectation of future capital appreciation to his land. In this situation, the zoning agency will be hard put in the interim to decide how to treat additional application for apartment development. In theory, as Neutze has pointed out,[55] the

---

[55] *Id.* at 43-47.

amount of prezoned land which is available can be used by the zoning agency as a control over the rate, sequence, and location of development. But the trouble is, as he recognizes, that entrepreneurs have different discount rates. Put more simply, some are willing to wait longer than others, and it is this variation in expectation which creates difficulties for the zoning agency.

Nor is the situation made any easier if the opposite occurs, and all of the land committed to apartments in any one area is utilized as rapidly as it is zoned. Here the problem is that developers seeking the capture of external economies in an area already committed to more intensive uses will put pressure on the zoning agencies to release additional land for apartments. But overdevelopment at any one point may in turn create serious problems for the total strategy, since development may not be attracted to other sectors in the planning area in which apartment development is also considered desirable.

Solutions to these problems are not simple. Policy dilemmas are created in any system in which the planning decision is separated from the development decision, and our free enterprise system has committed us to just such an arrangement in land development. But the point to make is that zoning must forever struggle with decisions that have both prospective and retroactive dimensions. To what extent should the zoning decision be based on what has already occurred in the marketplace, and to what extent should it be based on what ought to occur? Clearly the answer to this question will affect the level of uncertainty in the zoning process, and clearly the level of that uncertainty will in turn affect the landholding practices of land entrepreneurs and developers with whom the zoning system must deal. In our study of apartment rezonings in the Seattle metropolitan area we will see how one planning and zoning system dealt with these problems in practice.

### Development Timing and the Underutilization Problem

We have concentrated so far on the problems that arise from delays in developing more intensive apartment rezones which the zoning agencies have seen fit to give. Equally difficult problems in zoning control arise in those situations in which an

intensive land use has been indicated by the comprehensive plan
or zoning ordinance, but the market is not yet ready to respond
to the planning or zoning proposal at that level of development.
For example, suppose that the planning agency decides that an
optimum place for apartment development is a highway interchange area on the edge of its metropolitan area. It is also clear
that this area is not yet ready for such development. We have
indicated that it is in the community interest to forego development at a lower intensity now in the expectation of a more
intensive development later. Unfortunately, at least in the apartment development context, the municipality is rarely permitted
to make this decision. Given a taste preference hierarchy which
places single family development at the peak, and resultant zoning schemes which usually assume that single family development is always a permitted, residual use, the zoning agency may
not be able to defer single family development in anticipation
of a more intensive (and more desirable) multi-family use. It
may do so, of course, if it adopts a strategy of large lot zoning
as a device for deferring *any* development in a substantial seg-
ment of its jurisdiction. But zoning of this kind is suspect and
so far has not been heavily tested.[56] A more straight-forward
approach is simply to use the zoning process to reject an applicant on the ground that the area is more suitable for a more
intensive use. In economic terms, the municipality simply decides that the discounted value of the future use is at present
more valuable to the municipality than the present value of the
use for which a zoning change has been requested. What the
municipality has on its hands is a developer with a high discount
rate who cannot afford to wait out the uncertainty of the future return. My argument is that the municipality is entitled to
say that the developer's discount rate should be lower!

A classic case of this kind was presented in a recent Michigan decision, *Biske v. City of Troy.*[57] In this case, a suburban
municipality on the northern reaches of the Detroit metropol-

---

[56] *See* Comment, *Large Lot Zoning,* 79 Yale L.J. 1418 (1969).

[57] 6 Mich. App. 546, 149 N.W.2d 899 (1967), *rev'd in part on different grounds,* 381 Mich. 611, 166 N.W.2d 453 (1969). The writer happens
to have visited the site of this case and has supplied one or two additional
observations which are not apparent from a reading of the opinions.

itan area had prepared a land use plan which showed the site in question as part of a projected civic center and commercial complex. At present, the site is almost entirely undeveloped except for some municipal buildings. The applicant owned a lot at the corner of two secondary highways which were very close to an interchange on a new expressway. At two corners of this intersection were two relatively new filling stations. Not entirely the new look, but not decrepit either. The applicant applied for and was refused a zoning change to build yet another filling station. On appeal, the Michigan intermediate appellate court affirmed the municipality's decision, while the state's supreme court reversed.

Neither decision is particularly responsive to our problem. The appellate court, placing great faith in the planning process, felt that a contrary decision would simply gut the community plan. On the other hand, the supreme court was impressed with the fact that the plan was not adopted legislatively, and commented that the plan had not been realized by anything that had occurred on the ground. It was a dimension of reality that had no actualized existence, and the supreme court was not willing to credit it. In short, in the frame of reference we have been using, the community had engaged in a planning exercise in which it considered the externalities—here the external economies—as internal to its jurisdiction. It was willing to trade off investment opportunities in a balance which required one developer to defer the realization of present economies in the hope of future gain. The supreme court was unwilling to accept this strategy. It focused instead on the private tract as the unit of control, and applying a priority of occupation emphasis in a decision based on taste incompatibilities, it permitted the developer to capture his gain at a less intensive level of development. My point is that the supreme court's reaction is traditional. Had there been two existing residences at this intersection, my hunch is that the filling station developer would have been turned down. He would not have been allowed to visit externalities on these homeowners. The point was made earlier. Courts have had an easier time limiting and preventing external diseconomies than they have had in limiting and preventing the capture of external economies. A complete zoning policy requires both.

## Conclusion

We are now ready to move to an inquiry into the character and nature of the comprehensive plan, its role in the zoning process, and the court's evaluation of that role. But before we do we might summarize the trend of thought outlined in this chapter. We have taken an approach to the zoning process which emphasizes its role as a response to and correction of imperfections arising out of the private operation of the land market. This emphasis has started with the role of zoning in limiting and preventing the externalities arising from a pricing system which, left unaltered, has no method of forcing a calculation of externalities on the private entrepreneur. While we had started with the assumption that the identification of these externalities could be carried out under criteria which we might characterize as objective, we found in our discussion of the apartment zoning problem that even the regulation of land use incompatibilities carries with it a series of assumptions based on value choice. To better understand how these choices came to be made, we focused on the spatial frame of reference in which these choices are carried out. We found that in the traditional and neighborhood-based nuisance and zoning context, the courts (and the zoning ordinance) relied on existing patterns of development to provide a starting point for their evaluations.

No such convenient benchmark is available to guide the regulation of development opportunities in areas not yet developed. It was here, especially, that we found a more positive role for the planning and zoning process than the mere regulation of externalities at the neighborhood level. We took as our starting point Professor Kuhn's premise that the identification of external and internal values is definitional, and depends on the decisional locus within which the regulatory decision is made. We see a more positive role for the planning and zoning process in the allocation of positive development opportunities within the entire community, and when we shifted to this more positive role for zoning and planning the basis of land use allocations in value choices became even more explicit. The point was made in our urban limits example, and we noted that placing limits on the extent of urban development was the most important decision that had to be made by the planning system.

This concern with development opportunities at the community level also projects the planning and zoning process into the making of decisions which dimension the capital gain potential in land. How the zoning function is exercised, under what conditions of uncertainty the zoning allocation of land use is carried out, will in turn have important impacts on the price of land, on patterns of land holding and sale, and on the implementation of the municipality's zoning scheme.

# Chapter 3

## ZONING AND THE MANAGEMENT
## OF CHANGE

We are now ready to take a closer look at the detail of the zoning and planning process. We are interested in the legal techniques that have been made available for the implementation of the zoning power, and in how the comprehensive plan can provide guidance in the use of these techniques. Once more, we concentrate on development policies for urbanizing areas, using again our example of apartment zoning in suburbia, and we will find that the need to deal with the land market dynamics described in the last chapter has brought fundamental changes to the zoning system. Zoning, intended as a method for preallocating development opportunities, has been converted in urbanizing areas into an administrative system for managing environmental change, and which operates by responding to pressures for change as they occur in the marketplace. The methods for dealing with change, and the role of the comprehensive plan in providing a policy for change, engage our attention in this chapter. Because the courts are the tribunal of last resort for the zoning and planning process, we focus here on the judicial view of zoning change, and on the role of the comprehensive plan in justifying those changes under locally-adopted development policies.

*Zoning ". . . in accordance with a comprehensive plan"*

The initial enabling act for zoning provided that the zoning power must be exercised "in accordance with a comprehensive plan,"[58] and many of the state zoning statutes still contain this

[58] U.S. Dep't of Commerce, A Standard State Zoning Enabling Act § 3 (rev. ed. 1926) [hereinafter cited as Standard Act]. For discussion of the comprehensive plan see Black, *The Comprehensive Plan*, in W.I. Goodman & E.C. Freund, Principles and Practice of Urban Planning 349 (1968).

requirement. Unfortunately, the phrase was not made more explicit, and for that reason we have inherited to this day a long-standing confusion on just how the relationship between the plan and the zoning ordinance should be formulated.[59] Until recently, court decisions had generally made it clear that the phrase did not mean that the community had to have a published or adopted community plan, as distinguished from the zoning ordinance, and on which the zoning ordinance should be based.[60] Courts often found that the plan had been expressed in the policy of the very zoning ordinance which the plan was supposed to direct. Even more enlightening are cases which suggest that the statutory planning requirement is nothing but a statutory restatement of the conventional constitutional test, that any uncompensated exercise of the local regulatory power over private activities be reasonably exercised.[61]

The reasons advanced for this judicial emasculation of the statutory planning requirement have been many, and are often pragmatic, the most conventional being the point that many municipalities, especially the smaller ones, did not have plans until recently, and that to enforce the statutory requirement rigidly would have prevented municipal exercise of the zoning power. The explanation is suggestive, but it misses the point. What happened was that the courts were willing to accept the role of the zoning ordinance in adjusting land use interdependencies, but they were very reluctant to review the value preferences which the ordinance incorporated.[62] To have done so would have involved the judiciary in the political function of evaluating community goals, and this they were unwilling to do. A narrow judicial reading of the statutory requirement avoided an appraisal of the community value judgments expressed in the zoning ordinance, an interpretation buttressed by judicial adoption of the conventional presumption that the zoning ordinance was constitutional unless proved otherwise. Also of interest from this perspective are judicial interpretations of the comprehensive plan requirement which emphasize a comprehensiveness

---

[59] See T.J. Kent, The Urban General Plan 28-38 (1964).

[60] See Haar, In Accordance with a Comprehensive Plan, 68 Harv. L. Rev. 1154 (1955).

[61] E.g., Hadley v. Harold Realty Co., 198 A.2d 149 (R.I. 1964).

[62] See A.A. Altshuler, The City Planning Process 340-42 (1965).

in process as the essential component of the statutory test, rather than the substantive content of the plan's goals and objectives.

Recent statutory enactments[63] have given the comprehensive plan a more prominent place in the zoning process. For example, the Kentucky enabling act now provides that at least the preparation and adoption of land use objectives must precede the exercise of the zoning power.[64] Even apart from changes in statutory command, the more common preparation and availability of community comprehensive plans has forced the courts to give more attention to the role and function of the plan in zoning.[65]

We are interested here in these newer judicial attitudes toward the statutory comprehensive planning requirement, but we are interested as well in the impact of judicial interpretations on the conduct of the planning and zoning process at the local level. So we must begin by noting that confusions in the technology of zoning and planning have complicated the role of the plan in court decisions. One problem lies in a dispute over what form the comprehensive plan should take. Conventionally, the plan contained both a written statement and a map, and the way the model statute reads a map is apparently a compulsory part of the planning document. Now let us add that one aspect of the comprehensive planning process which is continually stressed by planning practitioners is its generality. As interpreted in the mapping of general plans, generality of intention is reflected in the preparation of land use plans at a big scale. Even neighborhood configurations are difficult to detect, much less the fine-grained adjustments that are required at the level of individual developments.

Generality of intention in mapping scale is also reflected in the usual tendency of the plan to employ land use groupings which are decidedly more generalized than the zoning district categories of the typical zoning ordinance. For example, while the zoning ordinance for a large city or urban county may have

---

[63] See Ark. Stat. 1947, § 19-2829; Ky. Rev. Stat., § 100.201.

[64] See Ark. Stat. 1947, § 19-2829; Ky. Rev. Stat., § 100.201.

[65] See S.J. Plager, Social Elements and Relationships Within Urban Systems: Implications for Action and Research Programs, The Role of Law (Sept. 1968Y.

as many as ten or fifteen zoning districts reflecting different densities of residential development, the general plan may be content with residential development areas shown at high, medium, and low densities. Translation of these generalized residential proposals into zoning districts is extremely difficult, especially since any one sector in the land use plan may cover an area so large that an infinite number of zoning district combinations may achieve the indicated density level.[66]

The important point to make next is that the zoning ordinance text is also accompanied by a map. But the zoning ordinance, as a legal control, is applicable to individual units of ownership, so the zoning map is drawn to the scale of these individual units and is much finer in grain than the comprehensive plan which accompanies and is supposed to guide it. We do not mean to imply that each individual lot is its own zoning district. The zoning district contemplated by the original zoning law might have included significantly large areas of the community, corresponding to the areas of significance isolated by the comprehensive plan. But the adoption of finely-divided categories in the zoning ordinance, the importance of the individual lot as a unit of legal control, and the legal necessity to respect existing and nonconforming uses, has meant that the zones as adopted by the zoning ordinance tend to be comparatively small and heavily mixed at any one point in the environment. As the Douglas Commission report pointed out,[67] the zoning act requires uniformity, but this requirement has been met by making regulations uniform within zones and by then mixing the zones on the zoning map.

We can now see the decision-making problem which is presented by the availability of both a land use plan map and a zoning map as an aid to the zoning process. The land use map of the comprehensive plan is a generalized indication of future land uses and densities. The zoning map is a detailed indication of legally permitted land uses at the scale of the individual ownership. How far the zoning ordinance categories of legally permitted uses should depart from the development that has

---

[66] *See* C.M. Haar, Land-Use Planning 730, 741 (1959).

[67] Report of the National Comm'n on Urban Problems, Building the American City 205 (1968).

already occurred presents problems that have never been faced directly. However that question is answered, the fact is that the contrast between the future land use and density proposals of the land use plan, and the presently permitted land use activities of the zoning ordinance, create tensions which are even more difficult to reconcile.

The problem is not helped, either, by the tendency of comprehensive plans to project a fixed "end state" as much as twenty to thirty years forward in time, with no attempt to indicate what zoning steps should be taken intermediate to the achievement of the goals ultimately projected. For example, plans seldom state a policy for development proposals which are less intensive than what the plan proposes—the problem of the *Biske* case. It is from this perspective that some critics have called for a more incremental and less far-ranging strategy for the planning process, with the planning function responding gradually over time to environmental problems as they arise.[68] Adoption of this kind of planning strategy would have important consequences for a planning technique which has emphasized static land use proposals, with little concentration on the problem of how to get from here to there.

Problems of implementation are most acute in undeveloped areas. We noted in the last chapter that the zoning ordinance has the greatest role to play in regulating development in areas not yet urbanized. Again, however, practice is not up to the opportunity. Partly for reasons already noted, zoning in undeveloped areas does not usually disturb the equilibrium of the land market by distributing development opportunities too far in advance of actual development. Instead, the zoning authorities often pursue a policy of watchful waiting, which they accomplish by zoning undeveloped areas to low intensity uses. The result is that zoning in undeveloped areas becomes a holding process in which the important zoning decisions are made by way of legislative and administrative change. Reliance on legislative and administrative techniques to make the important zoning decisions will in turn heighten the uncertainty that prevails in the zoning process, with effects we noted in the last

---

[68] *See* Lindblom, *The Science of "Muddling Through,"* 19 Pub. Ad. Rev. 79 (1959).

chapter. We should now observe that this emphasis in the zoning process also strengthens the role of the comprehensive plan as a guide to decisions by private developers. The point is a subtle one, but in the absence of existing development as an influence on the zoning pattern, and with widespread use of low intensity holding zones as the applicable zoning designation, it is the land use proposals of the comprehensive plan which have the greatest effect on the land market. The plan rather than the ordinance becomes the critical indicator of what the community expects in the way of development possibilities.

Now the fact that a land use map in a comprehensive plan assigns planning proposals to a physical location has proved troublesome in actual practice, partly because the physical location of land uses in advance has been self-defeating. We made the point earlier. Mapping an important corner for a shopping center, for example, will remove much of the uncertainty about future developmental possibilities, but will confer an immediate windfall on the owner of the land at that point. To the extent that the plan is a firm indication of public policy, the very certainty of the proposal will strengthen the holding power of the owner of the land at the time the plan was proposed, and the site may simply stay off the market. But certainty does not last forever in a dynamic urban environment, and the end state proposals which the plan projects will be qualified by intervening events, with limited capacity in the plan to respond to the change. In Seattle, Washington, for example, the unexpected commercial success of the jumbo jet, and the construction of a new Boeing factory, threw the projections of that area's transportation plan off base. As events qualify the land use proposals of the comprehensive plan, the certainty that any one site will in fact be used for the development that is indicated grows less.

Various techniques have been suggested to deal with these problems. Sites for major locators, such as shopping centers, have been shown schematically with several options open to would-be developers. This method helps, but it may only defer a difficult land use decision.[69] Other planning agencies have

---

[69] Tarlock, *Not in Accordance with a Comprehensive Plan: A Case Study of Regional Shopping Center Location Conflicts in Lexington, Kentucky,* 1970 Urban Law Ann. 133.

dropped the idea of a mapped plan altogether, and have experimented with the adoption of so-called policies plans in satisfaction of the demands of the planning process. The idea is that future land use proposals are not mapped. Instead, a set of written policies is adopted which provide general guidance to decision-making on individual zoning applications as they are presented for decision. These policies point to those environmental factors which should be influential in decisions on proposed developments, and in theory they mark an improvement over traditional technique because they avoid the problems of advance mapping which have been outlined above. From our point of view, however, from the point of view of the developer calculating the certainty or uncertainty with which a favorable development decision will or will not be made, the policies plan simply changes the statement form in which the land use intention is stated. Instead of a map indicating potential points of development, he has a statement of written policies which are not that difficult to translate into physical terms. For example, if the planning agency adopts a policy that apartment development should occur in the vicinity of highway interchanges, it takes a particularly dull developer not to realize that all the highway interchanges, proposed and otherwise, and which he can easily locate on the ground, are potential points for apartment development. One significant change is accomplished by the policies plan, nonetheless. Instead of having to deduce land development policies from a map of planning intentions, the developer now has before him a written statement of those policies which should become powerful weapons in any attempt to seek favorable action from the zoning agency. Moreover, the decision-making record of the zoning agency should give content to those policies as they are implemented in zoning decisions over a period of time.

## The Decision-Making Process in Zoning

We have seen that in urbanizing areas in which the zoning ordinance attempts no real allocation of land development patterns, and in which the zoning agencies pursue a policy of watchful waiting, land use decisions come to be made in response to pressures on the zoning system from individual developers. This shift in the nature of the zoning process has important consequences for the reception of the comprehensive plan, and to understand why this is so we must next turn to a more detailed examination of how that process operates. Here we face a tangled web indeed,[70] for the fact is that the decision-making structure contemplated by the standard zoning act has been distorted in practice by the demands of a system that simply could not work within the confines of the statute as it was initially proposed. The tale has been told before, but it needs brief recounting to give us perspective.

The structure of the standard zoning act really was quite simple. The legislative body of the municipality was to divide the municipality *in advance* into zoning districts. That was it, and that, in simple form, is what the statute authorizes. Unfortunately, the policy of watchful waiting which has especially been pursued in undeveloped and urbanizing areas has seriously qualified the use of advance zoning techniques, and has put the emphasis on zoning change in response to private development proposals as the dominant zoning mode. So it was the management of change that arose to bedevil zoning administrators everywhere. It was not that the act did not address itself to this problem. In a section aptly titled "Changes,"[71] the standard zoning act provided for "changes" to be made in the zoning ordinance by the legislative body, but no criteria for these changes were specified, probably because the decision to change is legislative and legislative decision-making needs no criteria. Moreover, and unfortunately, the key word "change" was not defined by the statute. This omission was intentional, though in a footnote the draftsmen did say that the term "it is believed will be construed by the courts to include 'amendments, supplements, modifications and repeal,' "[72] all of which are legislative actions explained to be necessary as a response to changing conditions or new conditions.[73] Note that no reference is made to a specific change in the ordinance which is based on the

---

[70] *See* Mandelker, *Delegation of Power and Function in Zoning Administration*, 1963 Wash. U.L.Q. 60, for a more detailed account.

[71] Standard Act § 5.

[72] Standard Act n. 31.

[73] Standard Act n. 30.

individual circumstances of the individual developer as presented in an individual application for development on an individual
tract. But it is just in this circumstance that the amendment
process has come most generally to be used. Not that the statute failed to realize that individual adaptations of the zoning
ordinance would be necessary. Another section[74] created a
Board of Adjustment which has two powers which concern us
here. One is to hear "special exceptions" from the terms of the
ordinance "upon which such board is required to pass under
such ordinance." Another is to authorize hardship variances
from the terms of the ordinance. While no explanatory foot-
notes indicate the scope of these powers, it is clear that they
were not intended to confer a generalized administrative power
to interpret and apply the zoning ordinance on a routine basis.

As all those familiar with zoning administration know, the
tail wags the dog. Routine techniques have developed under the
umbrella of the zoning statute which provide what is essentially
an administrative method for interpreting and applying the ordinance as applications for development arise. Some of these techniques are possibly subversive of the purposes of the ordinance,
and some are not. For example, in many communities variances
in "use" are granted by the board of adjustment to permit
deviations from the zoning regulations. This process is usually
considered subversive and is regularly condemned by all observers of the zoning scene. Another technique, considered less subversive, is to expand the concept of "exceptions" by creating an
administrative device under which changes in use can be allowed
subject to compliance with standards and conditions which are
explicitly stated in the ordinance. Power to grant these exceptions, or conditional uses as they are sometimes called, may be
given to the board of adjustment, to the planning commission,
or to the planning commission and the legislative body acting
together. But the sorry record of the board of adjustment in
bending (it is thought) too often to the pressures of developers
has encouraged the use of the planning commission as an alternative decision-making body. Conferring power on the planning
commission to exercise this power is startling to some because
the enabling act dealing with planning confers no such power,

---

[74] Standard Act § 7.

and legal difficulties sometimes arise.[75] The planning commission, under its statute, was only to have powers advisory to the legislative body in the planning process. This statutory function, however, has often been adapted to give the planning commission a decision-making role on individual applications for development.

This distortion of the statutory framework confronts the would-be developer with a bewildering array[76] of zoning possibilities when the zoning ordinance does not permit his development and he is required to seek a zoning change. He may go to the council to seek an amendment to the zoning ordinance authorizing his development. He may seek a hardship variance from the board of adjustment, though this avenue may be foreclosed if variances in "use" are prohibited in his jurisdiction. And he may seek an exception if it is authorized for his case. Note that the degree to which decisional criteria are made available for the zoning decision differs greatly depending on which technique is used:

1. In the amendment process,[77] no criteria are usually specified in the ordinance, and the only available controls are through an application of the policies of the comprehensive plan, or the policies dictated by the constitution to the extent that the courts are willing to review the amendment as a violation of Due Process or Equal Protection of the law. As we shall see below, however, the courts sometimes require that the need for a zoning amendment must be justified by changes that have occurred in the physical environment, or by changes in zoning policy.

2. In the variance process, the statutory test is "hardship," which is related to the restrictiveness of the zoning ordinance as compared to the proposed development. The variance was not intended to authorize changes based on generalized conditions in the environment as compared with conditions peculiar and individual to the tract in question.[78]

---

[75] *See* the discussion in Depue v. City of Clinton, 160 N.W.2d 860 (Iowa 1968).

[76] *See* Pettine v. Zoning Bd. of Review, 192 A.2d 433 (R.I. 1963).

[77] *But see* Ark. Stat. 1947, § 19-2829; Ky. Rev. Stat., § 100.201.

[78] Clarke v. Di Dio, 226 So. 2d 23 (Fla. Dist. Ct. App. 1969). For a case not permitting an apartment variance on the facts see Farah v. Sachs,

3. Only in the exception process are detailed criteria for zoning change specified. Now it may be noted that most developments for which an exception is authorized are marginal and usually troublesome cases which are difficult to handle under the more generalized rules of the zoning regulations. Hospitals in residential areas immediately come to mind. But the exception or conditional use procedure also has wider applications. In the context of our interest, it has been utilized for apartments,[79] and has become a technique for allowing the introduction of apartment developments into urbanizing areas previously committed to single family residential uses.

Sometimes zoning techniques are not even this clearcut. They may take hybrid forms, and we find just such an approach to decision making in a zoning ordinance which came before the highest New York court in the case of *Rodgers v. Village of Tarrytown.*[80] In what amounted to a hybrid zoning procedure, apartments were to be allowed in the one-family and two-family residential zones in the community subject to approval by the planning commission. Should the planning commission deny the application there could be an appeal to the governing body. No more than fifteen units were allowed in one apartment building, and a minimum tract size of ten acres was required. Detailed site, setback, and site coverage criteria were also imposed. These controlled the way in which the site was to be developed, in order to prevent any detrimental effect on surrounding land uses.

The Tarrytown ordinance illustrates a significant innovation in the management of change under the zoning ordinance. It not only bridges the more conventional techniques but, in the context of our apartment problem, illustrates some of the confusion in zoning over the role of use, density, and site treatment. To understand why this is so we must return to our analysis of the landmark *Euclid* opinion. There we wondered just what the concern of the United States Supreme Court was

---

10 Mich. App. 198, 157 N.W.2d 9 (1968). *But cf.* Kessler-Allisonville Civic League v. Marion County Bd. of Zoning Appeals, 137 Ind. App. 610, 209 N.E.2d 43 (1965).

[79] *See* Zieky v. Town Plan & Zoning Comm'n, 151 Conn. 265, 196 A.2d 758 (1963); La Rue v. Township of East Brunswick, 68 N.J. Super. 435, 172 A.2d 691 (App. Div. 1961).

[80] 302 N.Y. 115, 96 N.E.2d 731 (1951).

over the introduction of apartments in single family areas, and we asked whether the Court was concerned about density, site arrangements, use, or all of these. Indeed, harking back as well to our halfway house nuisance case, we wondered whether differences in living arrangements in residential dwellings could ever be generalized to the level of something called "uses," and which could serve as the basis of classification under zoning controls.

We see in the Tarrytown ordinance a compromise on these issues. As new apartment development under its provisions was effectively limited to single family zones, a limited though crude decision was made about the location of apartments within the community. Standards were also imposed on site development and these, together with the minimum tract size, worked to prevent any harmful effects on adjacent residences. Site controls, and a limitation on the number of units in each building, also put a ceiling on density. We would argue that all of these factors are important to zoning for apartment development, and that to characterize a zoning change for apartments as a change in "use" is much too simple. As we will see in our Seattle example, a zoning change to allow apartments may require attention both to density and to "use."

With this background in mind, we can now specify more concretely the zoning technique for allowing apartment development on which we intend to concentrate. Let us put aside the variance on the ground that it presents special problems, and that its use in apartment development is too problematic to justify close examination. We are left with the pure amendment, the pure exception or conditional use, and mixed forms such as the zoning technique employed in Tarrytown. Note immediately that formal differences between the legislative amendment and other methods should not hide the fact that, under all of these zoning approaches, there will be an application of development policies to the individual applicant who wishes to develop a particular piece of land. In the case of the conditional use or the Tarrytown hybrid, these criteria are spelled out in the ordinance. The amendment, on the other hand, may simply be carried out ad hoc, or we may have available a comprehensive plan which attempts to guide the amendment process. Differences in formalism should not obscure the fact that in each case the zoning agency is making a decision which may be guided by criteria adopted at the community level, whether expressed in the zoning ordinance or in the plan.[81] The only difference may be that in some jurisdictions the plan may not have been formally adopted by the local legislative body, while formal legislative adoption of the zoning ordinance is always required.

We concentrate on the amendment here because it provides the legal setting in which the plan is most likely to play a critical role. Zoning permissions for apartment development based on conditional use procedures, as in the *Tarrytown* case, turn on the criteria provided by the ordinance for their consideration. But enactment of the zoning amendment, like enactment of the initial zoning ordinance, must be "in accordance" with the comprehensive plan. So we look to the comprehensive plan to find meaning for the zoning amendment process.

In doing so, we must recall immediately the role we found for the comprehensive plan in making those developmental tradeoffs at the community level which may or may not be justified from the perspective of the more restricted neighborhood. We can illustrate the point by returning to our example of interchange development. If intensive apartment development is permitted in one quadrant of an interchange, then a persuasive argument can be made that the external economies flowing from that development should be subject to capture by would-be apartment developers in the other quadrants. If apartment development is limited to only one interchange quadrant, it must be on the basis of tradeoff decisions that have meaning at the community level, but not at the neighborhood level. We can see a basis for such a limitation if we will simply inspect our urban limits policies map which is reproduced in Chapter 2.

Unfortunately, when we turn to an analysis of the substantive basis for comprehensive planning judgments, we are sorely disappointed by what we find. As Dyckman has observed:

> The substantive norms of the physical plan have been subjected to little . . . scrutiny . . . . The fundamental approach dominates the physical planning solutions. The approved physical solu-

---

[81] De Meo v. Zoning Comm'n, 148 Conn. 68, 167 A.2d 454 (1961).

tions are marked by an enthusiastic tidying-up of land use mixtures, a restoration of more or less formal order, a segregation of uses, and the imposition of a middle-class aesthetic.[82]

Dyckman's observations strike home to us. We offer the observation that much of the zoning attention to apartment development has reflected the middle-class aesthetic to which Dyckman refers, as it has been motivated by a desire to exclude apartment development from those suburban and single family residential preserves in which the apartment is considered a violation of the environment. As a result, planning policies for apartments are caught in a crossfire. Often, as in the Tarrytown ordinance, there is a concern that apartments not be objectionable to neighbors. Thus, the restrictions on site coverage and development were part of the ordinance in that case. Concerns such as these speak more to the neighborhood scale, and are reminiscent of the approach taken in the nuisance cases. Elsewhere in the literature[83] much attention is given to community effects, and especially to the impact of apartments on tax revenues and school enrollments. These issues may especially agitate suburbanites who fear an apartment invasion, but their legitimacy as factors in zoning decisions is somewhat uncertain. We intend to focus instead on the larger question or urban development policies, and on the place of apartment development in the framework of a comprehensive plan which is sensitive to the allocation of development opportunities at the community level.

## Judicial Review of Zoning Change

Having examined the nature of the zoning process, and having noted the importance of the zoning change as a method of implementing zoning policy, we turn next to the role of the

---

[82] J.W. Dyckman, Introduction to Readings in the Theory of Planning: The State of Planning Theory in America 41 (unpublished manuscript, no date).

[83] For local studies see Bucks County Planning Comm'n, Apartments: An Analysis of Issues and Standards (June 1967); Woodbridge Dep't of Planning and Development, Garden Apartment Evaluation (Aug. 1968).

courts in reviewing zoning change and in assessing the impact of the comprehensive plan on the zoning decision. Our focus, as we have said, is on the zoning amendment, and on the use of the amendment to allow apartment development. Our discussion of the judicial attitude toward the zoning process, and the role of the comprehensive plan in that process, will provide necessary backdrop for our case study of the planning and zoning system in Seattle, Washington, to which we turn in our next chapter. The ultimate sanction for the zoning and planning process is in the courts, and what the courts will not accept the local community may not implement. But we should not be troubled by the possibility of judicial disfavor. We will find considerable ambiguity in court reception of the planning and zoning function, an attitude which leaves most of the options open to local planning and zoning authorities.

We must first note that the varied institutional response to managing zoning change has led to confusion, as the courts have been led astray by the formal legal basis on which zoning change has been allowed. They may take one kind of approach when reviewing conditional use or hybrid techniques, such as those employed in Tarrytown, and they may take a vastly different approach when dealing with zoning changes arising out of pure zoning amendments by the legislative body.

What happens is that the criteria for zoning change are formally specified in the ordinance which adopts a conditional use or hybrid procedure. In this instance, the court's function is closely defined. It may look at the application of the ordinance criteria to the case at hand. In the Tarrytown case, for example, a court could review to see if the criteria imposed by the ordinance had been satisfied. A court may inspect the acceptability of the criteria as well. In the field of filling station regulation, for example, the courts have been skeptical of zoning criteria which are based on the demand for filling station service in the locality, and will not usually accept a zoning procedure for filling station control which is based on this premise.

The amendment is more difficult. We have noted that the courts apply a presumption of constitutionality to legislative actions in zoning, and are extremely reluctant to look at the fairness with which zoning allocations are made much less the criteria on which they are based. When courts do intervene to review the zoning amendment they may be confused about their role. One problem is that a zoning amendment may appear to have singled out one developer for special treatment. A good example is our interchange situation which we discussed above. If one developer receives a zoning amendment for apartment development in one quadrant, why can't another developer likewise receive a zoning amendment for apartment development in another quadrant? The situation suggests favoritism and discrimination, and the courts are skeptical. They exhibit their skepticism by characterizing a rezoning of this kind as a "spot" zoning, with overtones that it is presumptively invalid. But judicial handling of these issues is often confused, and gets lost in the formalisms of the zoning system.

Some of these confusions are evident in a recent pair of Oregon cases, which were obviously considered by their court as the paragon of the model judicial approach. The cases are all the more interesting as the Oregon statute explicitly authorizes the enactment of zoning ordinances to "carry out" the comprehensive plan. In the first of these two cases, *Roseta v. County of Washington*,[84] neighboring landowners brought suit to test the constitutionality of a zoning amendment granted by the county board of commissioners. The rezone was granted to an owner of four lots who had already built an apartment on three of the lots before adoption of the zoning amendment. The classification on his fourth lot was changed by the rezoning from single family to multi-family use. This rezoning was invalidated. In reaching this result, the Supreme Court of Oregon reversed the usual zoning presumption. When passing on a zoning amendment, it held, the presumption of constitutionality would be reversed and the zoning agency would carry "the burden of proving that there has been a change in the neighborhood in order to justify the rezoning of a small tract as an amendment in keeping with the comprehensive plan."[85] This reversal of the usual presumption was adopted by the court as a cure to the evils of zoning, which the court found partly in the practice of granting requests at the behest of individual developers, and partly in a general failure to give effect to the comprehensive

---

[84] 458 P.2d 405 (Ore. 1969).
[85] *Id.* at 408.

plan. Even though there was evidence of other apartments in the area of the rezone, the county was held not to have met its burden of proof. Here we find judicial disfavor the "spot" zoning technique.

With Roseta should be compared its companion case of Archdiocese of Portland v. County of Washington.[86] This case considered a request for a conditional use permit to allow the construction of a church, school, and gymnasium in a residentially zoned area. The application for the conditional use had been denied by the county board of commissioners, and the denial was upheld by the Oregon supreme court. Roseta was distinguished, the court noting:

> [T]he ordinance [in the Archdiocese case] itself reveals the legislative plan forecasting the likelihood that certain specified uses will be needed to maximize the use of land in the zone for residential purposes. . . . Therefore, unlike the spot zoning cases the granting of permits for conditional uses is not likely to cause . . . [an] "erosive effect upon the comprehensive zoning plan."[87]

Apparently Oregon communities need only treat apartment developments as conditional uses in order to obtain the blessings of the Archdiocese opinion.

We might take several cuts at an explanation of what bothered the Oregon court in this pair of cases. Note first that the result in these cases did not depend on whether the municipality had acted favorably or unfavorably on the proposed development. We might expect, for example, that an allowance of a conditional use for a church and school would have been as much approved as a disallowance, apparently because the court favors the procedure under which the application was considered. Moreover, the court did not seriously trouble to look at the impact of its decisions on the immediate environment. Allowing additional apartment units in what was already a mixed

---

[86] 458 P.2d 682 (Ore. 1969).

[87] Id. at 686.

setting does not appear unreasonable, but the court upset a zoning amendment which did just that. Yet local exclusion of a church and school—a zoning action which has troubled courts elsewhere—did not receive judicial disapproval. We submit that the Oregon court has confused formalism with reality.

The court in *Roseta* was also worried about the ad hoc nature of the zoning change which the developer obtained. It explicitly disfavored rezoning on the basis of individual requests. Now this approach, if rigorously followed, would create real difficulties for a zoning system in which we have noted severe pressures which make zoning in advance less than workable, and which create a need for zoning agencies to respond to individual proposals as they are presented. The court in the *Archdiocese* case was not at all worried that the conditional use procedure employed there had formalized a method for passing on individual development proposals under criteria that had been specified in the ordinance. Why may the ordinance shift the initiative to the developer in the conditional use procedure, but not in the amendment process? Is there any real difference in the two situations? Other courts have thought not, and have been unconcerned about amendments to the zoning ordinance which came from the developer's initiative. In one Connecticut case, the comprehensive plan was changed to justify a zoning amendment on the same night to permit development by an individual landowner.[88] In Pennsylvania, administrative approvals of development have been almost contemporaneous with an amendment of the zoning ordinance creating the procedure under which the approval was given, and the court has not been troubled.[89] Even more interesting are the cases which recognize that a change in conditions surrounding the site in dispute can justify a departure from the comprehensive plan.[90] There is no limitation which disregards those changes which came about as a result of private initiative.

---

[88] Malafronte v. Planning & Zoning Bd., 155 Conn. 205, 230 A.2d 606 (1967). *See also* Westfield v. City of Chicago, 26 Ill. 2d 526, 187 N.E.2d 208 (1963).

[89] Cheney v. Village 2 at New Hope, Inc., 429 Pa. 626, 241 A.2d 81 (1968); Donahue v. Zoning Bd. of Adjustment, 412 Pa. 332, 194 A.2d 610 (1963).

[90] Furniss v. Township of Lower Merion, 412 Pa. 404, 194 A.2d 926 (1963).

Why should the court approve the private initiative which was authorized by the ordinance in the *Archdiocese* case, while disapproving the amendment which was granted to the developer in *Roseta*? The result in the *Archdiocese* opinion—exclusion of a religious school from a residential area—does not strike us as an occasion for wild applause, so that it would seem clear that the procedure so well received by the Oregon court does not necessarily guarantee a good zoning result. The court spoke of the role of the plan in *Roseta;* the Oregon statute is now comparatively strict in its insistence that zoning be based on a plan, and there was a plan in existence in the *Roseta* case. Why couldn't the plan in *Roseta* provide the same kind of guidance on community policy which the conditional procedure provision provided in *Archdiocese*? An argument was made that the plan in *Roseta* designated the area in controversy for residential use, which could have included either apartment or single family development. But the court dismissed this argument on the ground that the zoning ordinance made a zoning distinction between apartments and single uses. So it would seem that the court departed from its own severe injunctions about the value of the planning process, for it allowed the distinctions made by the ordinance to control the land use proposals made by the plan.

Moreover, the court ignored the fact that the very nature of the planning process leads to land use proposals that are more general than the zoning ordinance classification. Not to give meaning to the plan in view of this tendency is to dilute the effect of the planning process and give a superior position to the ordinance in spite of the statutory command that the plan has preference. We may decide later that the plan may have difficulty in providing this guidance, but that is a different matter than disregarding the plan altogether.

A very different role was accorded the plan in the case of *Cleaver v. Board of Adjustment*, a Pennsylvania decision.[91] This case arose in one of the Philadelphia suburbs. The municipality—one of the Pennsylvania townships which has been given extensive zoning powers—had rezoned the eleven-acre tract in

---

[91] 414 Pa. 367, 200 A.2d 408 (1964). For a history of planning activity in the Philadelphia suburbs see C.E. Gilbert, Governing the Suburbs (1967).

dispute from a single-family to a multi-family zone. Commercial zoning surrounding the property was cumulative, and permitted apartment construction, but the uses surrounding the tract could best be classified as institutional. The tract was bounded by a suburban railway station, a school, and a research center. In this instance the municipality had also prepared a comprehensive plan, which was a combination of mapped intentions and written policies. Thirty acres, including the rezone site, had been mapped in the plan for professional office use. This much detail is more than most plans might have provided. In addition, a written policy statement in the plan suggested that professional and apartment development be placed close to commuter railway stations. Note how the land use categories in the plan are more generalized than the typical land use categories in the zoning ordinance, although the court never reconciled the differences between the narrower land use indication of the planning map and the broader land use proposal in the written policies.

While the opinion is not entirely consistent, since it upheld the rezoning partly on the basis of the character of the uses surrounding the rezone site, it did in part discuss the effect of the comprehensive plan on the rezoning action. Here the opinion is worth quoting:

> It is clear that the Tredyffrin Land Use Plan (a) permits a defined range of choices in the zoning of appellant's property (as well as neighboring properties), and (b) *does not command* particular requirements of population density or setback or spacing for apartments thereon, and (c) clearly envisages and permits a proper zoning of the property here in question for apartments. [92] (Italics in original)

Neighboring owners had objected that the density of the apartments would be too high, and that setbacks would be insufficient. Neither of these questions had been addressed by the

---

[92] Cleaver v. Board of Adjustment, 414 Pa. 367, at 378, 200 A.2d 408, at 413 (1964).

plan, but the court was unwilling to force municipal attention to these problems. Instead, it was willing to credit the plan's decision that densities and setbacks were not important to the planning proposals. Had it been more sophisticated, the court might have said that a policy on density was implicit in the plan's decision to permit the location of apartments at the places and points indicated. But what is most significant is the court's emphasis on the "range of choice" permitted by the plan in the making of land use decisions. Here the court recognizes the role of the plan in guiding yet not constraining too tightly the development decision on apartment locations. The rationale of the case fits well with our concept of the planning and zoning process as a regulator of the certainty and uncertainty with which developmental expectations may be realized. The generality of the plan is a compromise on the uncertainty issue, but it requires more sophistication than the Oregon court exhibited to make a plan of this kind workable as a guide to zoning decisions.

### Third Party Interests and Judicial Review of the Zoning Function

In each of the cases we have just discussed a protest was made by neighbors to a zoning change which had been given to the applicant, and we must now observe that the nature of the judicial review function in zoning is closely affected by the way in which third party interests assert themselves in zoning litigation. We examined this problem in Chapter 1, but we must return to it here in order to see how the fact of a third party challenge affects the nature of the court's reviewing function, and especially its ability to inject the comprehensive plan into the zoning decision, as it did in the cases we have just discussed.

Once more, the problems grow out of the nature of the zoning technique which is utilized in passing on the developer's application. When the conditional use is employed, judicial review is limited to the ordinance criteria and the application of these criteria to the case at hand.[93] The interest of a potential

---

[93] Zieky v. Town Plan & Zoning Comm'n, 151 Conn. 265, 196 A.2d 758 (1963).

third-party litigant extends no farther, at least to the extent
that he is interested in the merits of the controversy. But in the
case of the pure amendment the legal position of the challenging neighbor may be on more tenuous ground. Just how the
challenging neighbor asserts his interest depends on what action
was taken on the developer's request, and on whether the developer himself chooses to appeal in the case in which he was
refused. There are three possibilities, depending on what action
is taken by the legislative body. (We are not complicating the
picture by discussing the exhaustion of remedies problem.)

In the simplest case, the property owner wishes to make a
use of his land which is not permitted by the zoning ordinance,
and brings an action against the zoning authority to have the
ordinance set aside as unconstitutional in its application to him.
He does not first attempt to secure an amendment to the ordinance to allow him to use the land as he proposes. In the second
case, the property owner requests an amendment, and has it
considered by the legislative body only to have the amendment
refused. Again, the action must be brought by the property
owner, and since the ordinance has not been changed to allow
his development, his legal attack will again be directed to the
unchanged ordinance as it is applied to him. In the final situation, the landowner has applied for his amendment and has
received it. He is not interested, of course, in court review, and
it is in this kind of case that neighboring property owners rise to
challenge the landowner's good fortune.

We might first note some preliminary problems in litigation
of this kind which affect in very important ways the court's
handling of the issues. We are referring here to the court of first
instance which gets the case, and not the state appellate court
which will review the decision of the lower court if it is appealed. It is generally the published opinions of the state appellate courts on which we rely for our zoning jurisprudence, but
the important point to make is that the kind of review which
the state appellate court can conduct is limited by the powers
of inquiry which were possessed by the court below which first
heard the case. What we have to ask about the lower court
proceeding is whether that court is bound by the record of what
has gone on before the legislative body that considered the
amendment, or whether the court may take additional evidence.

The court's power to take additional evidence is important, not only to a disappointed landowner who sought an amendment, but to a neighbor who challenges an amendment that was granted, or who intervenes in an action brought by the disappointed landowner who was not given what he asked.

Judicial reactions to this problem are tied up in some ancient and technical distinctions between the types of remedies that are available to review actions by local legislative and other bodies. For example, the State of Washington supreme court has been convinced that when the legislative body holds a hearing on the amendment, even if the amendment is denied, judicial review is by way of a special action known as certiorari. [94] In this kind of action, even the lower court is limited to a review of the "record" that has been made before the legislative body, and may not take new evidence. Moreover, strong presumptions of correctness apply to the action that is under review. [95] Other courts have held that the local zoning action by the governing body is legislative, at least to the extent that review is not by certiorari. [96] Additional evidence may then be taken by the lower court that hears the case. [97]

Limiting the reviewing court to the record may not be significant if the interested parties can build up an adequate record before the legislative body that hears the amendment. In practice, pressures of time, laxity in the conduct of the proceedings, and the absence of an adequate transcript limit the possibilities for doing so. When judicial review is by way of certiorari, the court may not usually probe further. [98]

As important as problems of evidence are to the scope and nature of judicial review in zoning actions, even more important constitutional problems arise in our third case, in which the landowner has been given his amendment and it is the neigh-

---

[94] Bishop v. Town of Houghton, 69 Wash. 2d 786, 420 P.2d 368 (1967).

[95] *Id.*

[96] Cascio v. Town Council, 158 Conn. 111, 256 A.2d 685 (1969); O'Rourke v. City of Tulsa, 457 P.2d 782 (Okla. 1969). *Cf.* Case v. City of Los Angeles, 218 Cal. App. 2d 36, 32 Cal. Rptr. 271 (1963).

[97] *E.g.,* Kort v. City of Los Angeles, 52 Cal. App. 2d 804, 127 P.2d 66 (1942) (allowing evidence of changed conditions).

[98] *See* the discussion in R.M. Anderson, American Law of Zoning § 21.04 (1968).

boring challenger who appeals. The problem is that when the amendment has actually been given the constitutional nature of the issues presented may lead the court to a different perception of its reviewing function. The difference lies in the fact that when the amendment has been denied, the restricted property owner may allege that the failure to allow him to capitalize on his development potential raises constitutional issues that can be conceptualized as a denial of property without Due Process of Law. When the case arrives before the court in this posture, the court is attracted to a viewpoint of the litigation which stresses the property owner's loss. When the property owner has been granted his rezone, the issue changes. In this case, the litigation is brought by neighboring challengers who assert that the rezone has been damaging to them. However, difficulties in finding a constitutional basis for the neighbor's lawsuit raise problems about the nature of the constitutional issue which courts are adjudicating when neighbors appeal.

These problems have been discussed at length by Professor Krasnowiecki.[99] He has suggested that neighboring property owners who challenge rezones have no constitutional basis for asserting their standing, and argues from the constitutional position of the neighboring landowner who, in eminent domain litigation, asserts that he has suffered compensable dàmage from the construction of a nearby improvement. Historically, the neighboring landowner's loss in these circumstances has been labelled as consequential and as constitutionally noncompensable. From this perspective, Krasnowiecki argues that neighbors should have no standing to question a rezoning in cases in which the objections to the rezone have a constitutional base. And in the amendment situation, if no ordinance criteria limit the amendment function, the neighbor's objection must rest on an allegation that some constitutional harm has been done to him.

This argument misses the point. For one thing, it misconstrues longstanding developments in condemnation law which provide a basis for awarding damages to complainants in situations in which the damage has historically been treated as conse-

---

[99] Krasnowiecki, *Planned Unit Development: A Challenge to Established Theory and Practice of Land Use Control,* 114 U. Pa. L. Rev. 3, at 47 (1965).

quential.[100] More important, it confuses the issue of standing with the issue of justiciability. Whether a litigant can participate in litigation is one matter; what issues he can raise is quite another. It is instructive that in cases in which the landowner challenges the unconstitutionality of an existing zoning ordinance as it has been applied to him, the courts treat the problem of intervention by neighbors in the lawsuit on strictly procedural grounds and are generally receptive to neighbor participation.[101] It would be unfortunate if courts were less lenient when the action is initiated by the neighboring challenger, even though there is a distinction, of course, between intervention in litigation already initiated and the initiation of litigation in the first instance.

Even accepting Krasnowiecki's analysis, we can find a constitutional basis for the neighbor's lawsuit which can result in comparable judicial treatment no matter how the litigation is started. In the language we have been using, the landowner finds a constitutional stance in an argument that the failure to rezone has limited him in capturing external economies which the environment affords him. The neighboring challenger finds his constitutional stance in the argument that the grant of a rezone has visited him with external diseconomies. If limitations on capturing increments in development value present the landowner with a potential constitutional issue, then the converse of this situation, the imposition of harmful externalities on neighbors, should equally be comprehended as a violation of a constitutionally protected interest. In other words, if the basis of zoning is the regulation of externalities, we should be able to find

---

[100] *See* Mandelker, *Inverse Condemnation: The Constitutional Limits of Public Responsibility*, 1966 Wis. L. Rev. 3. Krasnowiecki discusses this development but his dismissal of its impact is not satisfying. Krasnowiecki, *supra* note 99, at n.25. For discussion of this problem in the context of a zoning variance see Westling v. City of St. Louis Park, 170 N.W.2d 218 (Minn. 1969).

[101] *See* Weiner v. City of Los Angeles, 68 Cal. 2d 697, 441 P.2d 293, 68 Cal. Rptr. 733 (1968); Herzog v. City of Pocatello, 82 Idaho 505, 356 P.2d 54 (1960); Bredberg v. City of Wheaton, 24 Ill. 2d 612, 182 N.E.2d 742 (1962); Davidson v. Grosskopf, 128 Ind. App. 612, 150 N.E.2d 685 (1958); State *ex rel.* Algonquin Golf Club v. Lewis, 395 S.W.2d 522 (Mo. Ct. App. 1965); Application of Muccioli, 42 Misc. 2d 1088, 249 N.Y.S.2d 530 (Sup. Ct. 1964); Esso Standard Oil Co. v. Taylor, 399 Pa. 324, 159 A.2d 692 (1960).

constitutional issues present no matter which way the regulation cuts.

This digression to discuss the technicalities of standing to sue has important repercussions for judicial inquiry in zoning cases. If, as Krasnowiecki suggests, the neighboring challenger has no standing to assert the unconstitutionality of a rezone, then the court has no basis for intervention. On the other hand, if the neighbor does have standing then the court can be brought into the rezoning process. Nevertheless, the fact that the challenge is brought to a zoning amendment that has already been granted may have a profound effect on the litigation, for the court may be asked by challenging neighbors to consider the reasons which prompted the rezone. If it does, the court may be led to concentrate on the planning justification for the rezoning action rather than the loss of development value which would be suffered by the landowner were the rezone to be cancelled.

Perhaps reflecting the difficulties we have been discussing, the courts are simply not clear in deciding how to treat their review of a legislative rezoning. There are strong statements that the only justification for a rezone is found in the community plan.[102] On the other hand, many cases examine rezones on a narrower neighborhood scale without getting involved in the larger community issues.[103] The result is a confusion in which it is difficult to say just what the courts should be talking about in rezoning litigation. Let us examine the issues a little more closely. When a developer alleges the unconstitutionality of a zoning ordinance as applied to him, the courts are led by the nature of the constitutional allegation to concentrate on his loss of potential gain. At the same time, the courts are ambivalent about how to handle this claim of loss. On the one hand, they may dis-

---

[102] *See* De Meo v. Zoning Comm'n, 148 Conn. 68, 167 A.2d 454 (1961); Strandberg v. Kansas City, 415 S.W.2d 737 (Mo. 1967); Walus v. Millington, 49 Misc. 2d 104, 266 N.Y.S.2d 833 (Sup. Ct. 1966); Place v. Hack, 34 Misc. 2d 777, 230 N.Y.S.2d 583 (Sup. Ct. 1962). *Compare* Zoning Comm'n v. New Canaan Bldg. Co., 146 Conn. 170, 148 A.2d 330 (1959) (upzoning).

[103] *E.g.*, City of Little Rock v. McKenzie, 239 Ark. 9, 386 S.W.2d 697 (1965); Central Ky. Dev. Co. v. Bryan, 416 S.W.2d 743 (Ky. Ct. App. 1967); Gratton v. Conte, 364 Pa. 578, 73 A.2d 381 (1950); Toole v. May-Day Realty Corp., 223 A.2d 545 (R.I. 1966).

count the potential for gain by pointing out that a reduction in capital value is the consequence of any zoning ordinance which restricts the landowner's development opportunities.[104] Indeed, this point was made in the *Euclid* case. On the other hand, when the deprivation goes too far the courts are likely to talk of a "confiscation" of the landowner's property which leads to a finding that the zoning ordinance as applied is unconstitutional.[105] We are not told, however, just where the line should be drawn, and we have pointed out that deprivation of value as a test of unconstitutionality has serious weaknesses.

When a rezone has been granted to the developer, we usually find an argument that the zoning is a "spot" zoning which is invalid. But just what makes the spot zoning unconstitutional is not clear, and we did not get much guidance from our Oregon cases. Is it the size of the area rezoned? Many observations to this effect appear in the cases, and a judicial preference for large rezones supports our own observations that larger tracts permit the developer to internalize his externalities and take advantage of the size of the site to protect neighbors from harmful consequences. The thought also appears that the spot zone is arbitrary, that a denial of Equal Protection in the constitutional sense occurs because the developer is allowed a rezone in circumstances in which it is denied to others. Then the comment is made that the rezone can be justified and these objections overcome, but only provided the rezone is found to be justified in the community interest. When this approach is taken, reliance on the comprehensive plan as an expression of that community interest is made explicit.[106] What the courts are saying is that they will examine the development tradeoffs that have been made at the community level to determine if the policy underlying the rezoning decision justifies the rezone at the specific site, and forecloses the allegation that the rezone arbitrarily favors the fortunate developer. Nothing prevents the courts from making the same kind of inquiry when the issue is a denial of a zone change to the developer, but the concentration on the

---

[104] Krause v. City of Royal Oak, 11 Mich. App. 183, 160 N.W.2d 769 (1968).

[105] Summers v. City of Glen Cove, 17 N.Y.2d 307, 217 N.E.2d 663, 270 N.Y.S.2d 611 (1966).

[106] *See* case cited note 45 *supra.*

developer's alleged deprivation of property without Due Process probably diverts the court's attention from the larger issues. Here Krasnowiecki is probably right when he suggests that the less familiar nature of the neighboring challenger's interest when he attacks a rezone probably leads the court to focus on the community impact of the rezone, rather than the alleged deprivation to the landowner.

## Judicial Response: The "Law" of Apartment Zoning

We might now examine the principles that the courts have developed when reviewing zoning amendments for apartment development. That our inquiry will not be mightily productive has already been indicated. We must rely on the opinions of appellate courts for guidance, and their review will be limited factually by what went on both before the legislative body and the court below. The application of the usual presumption of constitutionality to legislative zoning amendments, contrary to the position of the *Roseta* case, further weakens the substantive contribution which courts are able to make. Often they are content with affirming the legislative action on the ground that the legislative judgment is reasonably debatable.

Moreover, our discussion of the basis for judicial intervention in zoning controversies has suggested that the courts will be confused about the scope of their review. To be precise, they will be undecided whether to review apartment zoning with reference to the guidelines of the comprehensive plan, or whether to evaluate apartment zoning under the more limited externality tests which zoning inherited from the nuisance cases. A review of the apartment zoning cases indicates the nature of this confusion. Zoning imported from the nuisance cases a simple model of residential development based on a taste hierarchy in which single family residences stand at the peak. Apartments are accorded a secondary buffer role between the preferred single family use and other uses, which are supposedly even more obnoxious to the single family home dweller. References to the buffer role for apartments appear throughout the cases,[107] and

---

[107] *E.g.*, City of Little Rock v. McKenzie, 239 Ark. 9, 386 S.W.2d 697 (1965); Evanston Best & Co. v. Goodman, 369 Ill. 207, 16 N.E.2d 131

lead to a judicial emphasis on the immediate neighborhood as the spatial referent in which apartment zoning is evaluated. Externalities are examined in this framework, as in the nuisance cases. The rezoning approved by the Pennsylvania court in the *Cleaver* opinion is an excellent example of a planning policy which explicitly recognized the buffer function. Perhaps it was this treatment of apartment zoning which led the Pennsylvania court so readily to accept the comprehensive plan as a guiding document for zoning regulation.

On the other hand, we are also interested in the role which the comprehensive plan can play in making allocations for apartment development. Unfortunately, we are not always sure whether the plan has made these allocations on the basis of a community policy, or merely in order to prevent incompatibilities in neighborhood development. The plan in *Cleaver* is in this category. These confusions sometimes make the judicial perspective difficult to characterize. Floating through the cases, for example, are references to the need for apartments as a justification for the apartment rezone.[108] Apartment need can be used as the basis for a location policy which can override local objections based on allegedly harmful impacts. But the planning implications of a "need" test are never fully articulated. Moreover, land use regulation based on need suggests restriction in the name of allocating competitive opportunities. This issue demands our attention, and we put it aside in these pages only in

(1938); Central Ky. Dev. Co. v. Bryan, 416 S.W.2d 743 (Ky. Ct. App. 1967). *See* Zandri v. Zoning Comm'n, 150 Conn. 646, 192 A.2d 876 (1963). This and other myths surrounding the apartment zoning process are discussed in Babcock & Bosselman, *Suburban Zoning and the Apartment Boom*, 111 U. Pa. L. Rev. 1040 (1963), and in *Apartments in Suburbia: Local Responsibility and Judicial Restraint: A Symposium*, 59 Nw. U.L. Rev. 344-432 (1964). *See also* American Soc'y of Planning Officials, Planning Advisory Service, Information Rep. No. 187, *Apartments in the Suburbs* (1964); L.A. Syracuse, *Arguments for Apartment Zoning* (Nat'l Ass'n of Home Builders, Information Bull. No. 1, 1968) (extensive review of the literature). Underlying the buffer approach, of course, is the judicial inheritance from *Euclid* which treats the apartment as a harmful invading use. This point is made in the articles cited above. *See, e.g.,* Fanale v. Hasbrouck Heights, 16 N.J. 320, 139 A.2d 749 (1958).

[108] *See* Malafronte v. Planning & Zoning Bd., 155 Conn. 205, 230 A.2d 606 (1967); Pierrepont v. Zoning Comm'n, 154 Conn. 463, 226 A.2d 659 (1967); George LaCava & Sons, Inc. v. Town Plan & Zoning Comm'n, 154 Conn. 309, 225 A.2d 198 (1966); Strandberg v. Kansas City, 415 S.W.2d 737 (Mo. 1967); Schadlick v. City of Concord, 108 N.H. 319, 234 A.2d 523 (1967).

order to focus on the allocation of apartment zoning in the name of more traditional planning objectives.

Equally difficult to characterize are judicial references to improvements in highways and in highway access as a justification for apartment zoning. On the one hand, the court may be concerned that higher density apartment uses have sufficient access to the highway network, perhaps reflecting an assumption that apartment dwellers hold down more jobs per unit because they are often older or younger couples without families, or singles. Or the court may simply be concerned that apartment development be present to buffer any single family residences from the noises and fumes of the highway. If this is the concern, then the court is more interested in the immediate impact of the highway than in the effect of the highway on community structure and development.

### Judicial Response: The Maryland Cases

In looking for a body of court cases which can give us an insight into judicial attitudes toward zoning change for apartment development, we can find our best lead in the significant number of apartment zoning decisions which have been decided by the Maryland Court of Appeals, the highest appellate court in Maryland, and that have arisen largely in the suburban areas surrounding Washington, D.C., and Baltimore. These cases deal almost entirely with zoning amendments, and requests for zoning amendments. The Maryland cases reflect some of the ambivalence which we have found in our discussion of judicial review of zoning change, for they are partly attentive to the impact of apartment development on neighborhood patterns, and partly responsive to the influence of the comprehensive plan on the zoning amendment process.

Fortunately for our inquiry, the Maryland suburbs around Washington have been blessed by a local government pattern in which the usual role of incorporated suburban municipalities has been minimized. There are few incorporated suburbs of note, and the zoning authority has been lodged with two suburban counties, Montgomery and Prince Georges. These counties have been jointly served by the Maryland National-Capital Park and Planning Commission, which functions in the manner of a subregional planning agency. Whatever policy has been adopted for planning and for apartments, therefore, is uniform throughout the Maryland side of the Washington suburban area, with the exception of a few incorporated municipalities which lie outside the jurisdiction of the Commission and which do their own zoning.

Moreover, the regional planning agency for the entire Washington area adopted, in 1961, a regional plan which outlined a framework of development for the entire region. Called the *Year 2000 Plan*, [109] it proposed a series of high density centers located in corridors radiating out from the urban core. On the Maryland side a supplemental plan, *On Wedges and Corridors*, [110] implemented the proposals of the *Year 2000 Plan* for the Maryland portion of the Washington region which is under the jurisdiction of the Maryland National-Capital Park and Planning Commission. Whether or not the far-reaching proposals contained in the *Year 2000 Plan* and in *Wedges and Corridors* have been implemented is another question, [111] but whatever the success of the regional planning effort, individual local plans have been and are being prepared by the Park and Planning Commission for various sectors of Montgomery and Prince Georges Counties. Some of these precede and some are subsequent to the *Wedges and Corridors* plan. These local plans cover relatively small areas, and are considerably more detailed than we might expect a comprehensive plan to be. For example, they are detailed enough to show planning proposals for major intersections and highway interchanges. This background should be kept in mind when examining the Maryland court cases discussed below. Dissatisfaction with such detailed planning has now led to proposals for more generalized land use plans. It would also appear that planners in the Maryland suburbs were caught short without a policy for the suburban apartment boom

---

[109] National Capital Planning Comm'n-National Capital Regional Planning Council, A Policies Plan for the Year 2000: The Nation's Capital (1961).

[110] Maryland-National Capital Park and Planning Comm'n, On Wedges and Corridors: A General Plan for the Maryland-Washington Regional District (1964).

[111] For a critique see Metropolitan Washington Council of Governments, The Changing Region: Policies in Perspective (1969).

that began around 1960, and handled apartment rezonings ad hoc.[112] Nevertheless, as a consequence of the simplified governmental structure and the extensive planning activity of a subregional planning agency, the Maryland counties outside Washington have been provided with as intensive a planning program as any that can be found in the United States. Planning outside Baltimore has been handled by an equally powerful planning agency serving Baltimore County, which also has few incorporated cities, and the regional planning effort here appears almost as intensive as in the Washington suburbs.[113]

To understand the legal posture of apartment rezoning cases from these counties as they reach the Maryland Court of Appeals, we must next look at the way in which rezonings are granted. At the time most of the cases under review were decided, the planning staff in Montgomery and Prince Georges Counties made an initial recommendation to the planning commission, which then decided to grant or to deny the rezone. The county council of the county concerned then acted on the recommendation of the planning commission, with a further appeal (if desired) to the lower (circuit) court and then to the appellate court. In Baltimore County the procedure is similar, except that the initial zoning decision is taken by a zoning commissioner with a further appeal available to the county board of zoning appeals, subject to a final appeal to the courts. In the Washington suburbs the rezoning procedures fit the usual pattern. In Baltimore County the agencies involved are somewhat atypical, although the effect of the zoning action is the same. What is most important is that the Maryland courts, when faced with a zoning case, find themselves either passing on a legislative rezone or on a refusal to grant the rezone that has been requested.

Over fifty zoning cases dealing with apartment zoning amendments and requests for amendments have been decided

---

[112] *See* G.M. Neutze, The Suburban Apartment Boom 45 (1968), suggesting that apartment rezonings in the Maryland suburbs were easy to get in the 1963-1966 period.

[113] *See* Baltimore Regional Planning Council, Comprehensive Plan: Projections and Allocations for Regional Plan Alternatives (August 1965). For a general discussion of planning and zoning in these areas see Maryland Planning and Zoning Law Study Comm'n, Interim Report 34-37, 42-55 (Jan. 1968).

by the Maryland Court of Appeals in the past five years, a rich decisional pool which permits some analysis of the basis of decision in zoning litigation. Unfortunately, as we might have expected, the ad hoc nature of the court's decisions and its failure to articulate its zoning policies carefully has led to considerable confusion. For example, the court has acknowledged that cases in which the landowner appeals from a denial of a rezoning differ from cases in which neighbors appeal from a grant of a rezoning.[114] But a close analysis of the cases would suggest that the issues in the two cases are about the same. Thus the familiar presumption of constitutionality accorded a legislative judgment applies both to a denial and a grant of a rezoning.[115] Nevertheless, in cases in which the rezoning has been denied, the court has concentrated on the taking issue—whether or not there has been a constitutional taking of the owner's property—more so than it has in cases in which the rezone has been granted.[116] In denial cases, the court has also said that the landowner faces a harder burden of proof.[117] On balance, however, a lack of clarity in the decisions leads us to treat both situations as the same.

Another peculiarity in Maryland zoning jurisprudence also needs to be noted. In most jurisdictions, a rezoning may be justified by a change in zoning policy as well as a change in environmental physical conditions which are alleged to justify the rezone.[118] In Maryland, a rezoning is justifiable only if there has been a mistake in the original zoning, or a change in the physical conditions on which the zoning was premised. Whether the so-called Maryland change-mistake rule is more lim-

---

[114] Park Constr. Corp. v. Board of County Comm'rs, 245 Md. 597, 227 A.2d 15 (1967).

[115] *Id.*

[116] Pallace v. Inter City Land Co., 239 Md. 549, 212 A.2d 262 (1965); DePaul v. Board of County Comm'rs, 237 Md. 221, 205 A.2d 805 (1965).

[117] Board of County Comm'rs v. Meltzer, 239 Md. 144, 210 A.2d 505 (1965).

[118] *See* MacDonald v. Board of County Comm'rs, 238 Md. 549, 210 A.2d 325 (1965), especially the dissenting opinion. For discussions of zoning problems in Maryland see A.H. Rathkopf, Law of Zoning and Planning ch. 27, § 1 (3d ed. 1969); Goldman, *Zoning Change: Flexibility v. Stability*, 26 Md. L. Rev. 48 (1966); Liebman, *Maryland Zoning—The Court and Its Critics*, 27 Md. L. Rev. 39 (1967).

iting in theory than in practice may be open to question. For our analysis, the important point is that the Maryland court's concentration on physical change leads it to consider the compatibilities and incompatibilities which are important in an application of the buffer concept in apartment zoning.

Recent decisions permit the Maryland court greater freedom with ordinances which create what are known as floating zones. These ordinances often provide for approval of apartments under a procedure similar to those used in *Tarrytown*.[119] A zone is created by the ordinance which "floats" until application is made and approval given by the local zoning authority, under criteria which may go beyond the change-mistake rule. But the Maryland court still insists[120] that the approval of a floating zone requires a compatibility finding, an attitude which forces an appraisal of the surroundings in which the floating zone is to be placed. To this extent, the floating zone cases present issues similar to the more conventional rezone cases, except that an explicit finding of "change" is not required. Whenever the floating zone cases provide a basis for appraising the court's attitude toward land use compatibilities in apartment zonings, they will be discussed here.

But we focus primarily on zoning amendments. As we have seen, a zoning amendment will be upheld if it is reasonably debatable, and so it is difficult to abstract from the cases any sense of the "law" of zoning as it is applied to apartment development. What is possible, however, is to isolate those environmental factors to which the court gives weight in deciding whether the presumption has been overcome, and in deciding whether the requirements of the change-mistake rule have been met. From an analysis of these environmental factors, and the weight which the court gives them, we ought to be able to develop some sense of the criteria which the court uses in deciding when apartment development is compatible with its surroundings.

---

[119] Bujno v. Montgomery County Council, 243 Md. 110, 220 A.2d 126 (1966). *See* Beall v. Montgomery County Council, 240 Md. 77, 212 A.2d 751 (1965).

[120] Bigenho v. Montgomery County Council, 248 Md. 386, 237 A.2d 53 (1968).

When making this appraisal, however, we face ambiguities in the decisions about the role of the comprehensive plan. Some years have elapsed in both the Baltimore and suburban Washington areas since the last adoption of their initial zoning ordinance. The cases thus present the comparatively simple issue of the effect on an initial zoning of changes in the environment which have occurred since the initial zoning was adopted, or since the zoning ordinance was last totally revised. On this issue the Maryland court has done a careful dance. Major highway improvements which had been contemplated by the land use plan were not enough to show a "change" which would justify a rezoning.[121] On the other hand, the land use proposals of the plan do have weight, for general adherence in the zoning process to the land use proposals of the plan is a factor to be considered in denying a rezoning which is contrary to the plan.[122] But adoption of the land use plan subsequent to the zoning ordinance, while a factor to be considered by the zoning agency, does not give rise to a presumption of change when the land use allocation of the plan differs from the zoning classification. [123] The court has emphasized that the long-range focus of the plan is not necessarily binding on the short-range zoning judgment.[124] At the same time, the adoption of a new conditional use, floating zone, or planned development procedure subsequent to the adoption of the plan is considered an updating of the plan, the court pointing out that otherwise the plan must be changed if changes in land use are to be achieved.[125] Just how a change in the zoning ordinance can be considered a change in the plan is not made clear, unless the court means to take the view that the criteria for approval which are stated in the floating zone procedure are a substitute for the land use criteria

---

[121] Chatham Corp. v. Beltram, 252 Md. 578, 251 A.2d 1 (1969).

[122] Board of County Comm'rs v. Farr, 242 Md. 315, 218 A.2d 923 (1966). Cf. Sampson Bros., Inc. v. Board of County Comm'rs, 240 Md. 116, 213 A.2d 289 (1965).

[123] Board of County Comm'rs v. Edmonds, 240 Md. 680, 215 A.2d 209 (1965).

[124] Board of County Comm'rs v. Kay, 240 Md. 690, 215 A.2d 206 (1965). Cf. Montgomery v. Board of County Comm'rs, 261 A.2d 447 (Md. 1970).

[125] Bigenho v. Montgomery County Council, 248 Md. 386, 237 A.2d 53 (1968).

contained in the plan. This position appears to echo the Oregon court's holding in the *Archdiocese* case.

We will attempt a more satisfactory appraisal of the Maryland court's attitude toward the influence of the comprehensive plan on zoning by examining a series of cases which arose, over a brief span, at one location in Montgomery County. Before we can do so, however, we must return to the more restricted neighborhood focus on apartment zoning in an attempt to determine how the court views the pattern of externalities at this level as it affects the zoning judgment. Conflicting statements[126] appear in the opinions on the importance to the zoning decision of the need for apartments, either in the immediate area or in the county, and we will not say more on this issue. More typically, the court's attention is drawn to development patterns. In explanation of the change-mistake rule, the court has held that close-in changes near the site of the proposed apartment may be used to justify the rezoning,[127] but that changes that are too distant may not.[128]

Perhaps it is best to state, in sequence, the criteria which the Maryland court uses in making operational its notions of the neighborhood characteristics which can support apartment rezonings. In evaluating the comments that follow, please keep in mind that the Maryland apartment zoning cases, like most zoning cases, are decidedly ad hoc. We are not suggesting that the factors we have isolated are determinative of the zoning result. We are only isolating factors which appear to enter into and weigh on the court's decision.

1. Like many courts, the Maryland court accepts the principle that apartments may and should be used as buffers between single family residential development and the more intensive and supposedly less desirable nonresidential users.[129]

---

[126] That need is a factor to be considered see Finney v. Halle, 241 Md. 224, 216 A.2d 530 (1966). *Contra*, Pahl v. County Bd. of Appeals, 237 Md. 294, 206 A.2d 245 (1965); Shadynook Improvement Ass'n, Inc. v. Molloy, 232 Md. 265, 192 A.2d 502 (1963).

[127] Bayer v. Siskind, 247 Md. 116, 230 A.2d 316 (1967). *Cf.* O.F. Smith Bros. Dev. Corp. v. Montgomery County Council, 246 Md. 1, 227 A.2d 1 (1967).

[128] Randolph Hills, Inc. v. Whitley, 249 Md. 78, 238 A.2d 257 (1968).

[129] Brown v. Wimpress, 250 Md. 200, 242 A.2d 157 (1968); Wahler v. Montgomery County Council, 249 Md. 62, 238 A.2d 266 (1968). *Cf.* Bishop v. Board of County Comm'rs, 230 Md. 494, 187 A.2d 851 (1963).

2. However, permitting an apartment rezoning as an appropriate buffer does not justify the extension of that buffer in a subsequent rezoning.[130] This viewpoint justifies the zoning agency if it wishes to limit the continued capture of external economies in a developmental situation. Unfortunately, the basis for making this judgment is not made clear by the court, other than a relatively crude inference that one bite at the environment is enough.

3. Undeveloped apartment rezonings in the area of the rezone site justify the zoning agency's refusal of another apartment rezone in the same area.[131] In terms of our analysis, this principle enables the zoning agency to achieve some control over the supply of rezoned land in the land market. But it would seem to create zoning dilemmas in those areas in which the market underresponds, but the zoning agency considers additional apartment zoning to be in accord with the plan. Perhaps the answer is that the court leaves the options open in this situation and does not demand a refusal.

4. Highways are proper boundaries between areas of more intensive and less intensive land use.[132] So are interchanges on limited-access highways.[133] Applying this precept, the court accepts a major traffic artery as a boundary to mark off the "neighborhoods" within which the court's analysis of the character of the environment will take place. But we should repeat our initial confusion over the use of apartment development to insulate the externalities produced by the highway, and the importance of accessibility to the highway network as a factor in planning the larger community. However, a highway counts as a change in condition which justifies apartments, as the next paragraph indicates.

---

[130] Brown v. Wimpress, 250 Md. 200, 242 A.2d 157 (1968); Wahler v. Montgomery County Council, 249 Md. 62, 238 A.2d 266 (1968); Randolph Hills, Inc. v. Whitley, 249 Md. 78, 238 A.2d 257 (1968); Baker v. Montgomery County Council, 241 Md. 178, 215 A.2d 831 (1966); Levy v. Seven Slade, Inc., 234 Md. 145, 198 A.2d 267 (1964).

[131] Park Constr. Corp. v. Board of County Comm'rs, 245 Md. 597, 227 A.2d 15 (1967); Board of County Comm'rs v. Edmonds, 240 Md. 680, 215 A.2d 209 (1965).

[132] Agneslane, Inc. v. Lucas, 247 Md. 612, 233 A.2d 757 (1967); Bujno v. Montgomery County Council, 243 Md. 110, 220 A.2d 126 (1966); Stockdale v. Barnard, 239 Md. 541, 212 A.2d 282 (1965).

[133] Kaslow v. Mayor & Council of Rockville, 236 Md. 159, 202 A.2d 638 (1964).

5. The construction of a new highway or major thoroughfare in the vicinity of the rezone site is a change in condition favorable to the granting of an apartment rezone.[134] So is a substantial street improvement,[135] although the construction of a secondary road is not.[136] On the other hand, proposals for new highways, such as Interstate highways, are not enough. [137] However, the highway proposal may be considered if its execution is reasonably probable, and if it means a basic change in the character of the neighborhood.[138]

Concern with immediate externalities appears in the next set of propositions.

6. A very large tract is its own neighborhood, and internal compatibilities of use are as important as the external relationship of the site to its surroundings.[139] Any adverse external impacts can be handled through the site plan approval process for the entire site.[140] These statements appear principally in floating zone cases in which review and approval of the entire site is part of the zoning process. Nevertheless, this approach to rezoning merely echoes the sensible conclusion, advanced earlier, that if external diseconomies are the regulatory problem in zoning, they can be handled better by developers who control a large enough site to internalize the externalities they create. This point has been emphasized[141] by the Maryland court's

---

[134] Ragan v. Hildesheim, 247 Md. 609, 233 A.2d 761 (1967); Beth Tfiloh Congregation v. Blum, 242 Md. 84, 218 A.2d 29 (1966); Finney v. Halle, 241 Md. 224, 216 A.2d 530 (1966).

[135] Jobar Corp. v. Rodgers Forge Community Ass'n, 236 Md. 106, 202 A.2d 612 (1964).

[136] Board of County Comm'rs v. Kines, 239 Md. 119, 210 A.2d 367 (1965).

[137] Park Constr. Corp. v. Board of County Comm'rs, 245 Md. 597, 227 A.2d 15 (1967); Board of County Comm'rs v. Meltzer, 239 Md. 144, 210 A.2d 505 (1965). Contra, Bujno v. Montgomery County Council, 243 Md. 110, 220 A.2d 126 (1966).

[138] Brenbrook Constr. Co. v. Dahne, 254 Md. 443, 255 A.2d 32 (1969); Jobar Corp. v. Rodgers Forge Community Ass'n, 236 Md. 106, 202 A.2d 612 (1964); Rohde v. County Bd. of Appeals, 234 Md. 259, 199 A.2d 216 (1964).

[139] Bigenho v. Montgomery County Council, 248 Md. 386, 237 A.2d 53 (1968); Board of County Comm'rs v. Turf Valley Associates, 247 Md. 556, 233 A.2d 753 (1967).

[140] Bigenho v. Montgomery County Council, 248 Md. 386, 237 A.2d 53 (1968).

[141] Id.

refusal to apply the change-mistake rule in the floating zone cases, where compatibility is the test. But we are still left troubled by this explanation. It is true that legal difficulties under the more conventional amendment procedure may make it difficult to condition a legislative amendment with administrative review of the site plan,[142] a process which is essential if the developer's handling of his site in relation to the surrounding area is to be properly evaluated. This difficulty can be avoided by a shift to an administrative process which can include site plan review, as under the Maryland floating zone procedure. However, a major change in the character of development still results whenever the floating zone technique is employed to introduce apartments into residential areas, and the more liberal treatment of the floating zone procedure by the Maryland court simply hides this reality. Zoning change to introduce apartment development is therefore less rigorously treated by the court when it occurs by way of a floating zone than by way of a conventional zoning amendment, a troublesome interpretation unless the Maryland court means that change is only difficult because of the externality problem, and that the externalities can be handled adequately on the large tracts, subject to site review.

7. A mere increase in traffic and in school population does not justify denial of an apartment rezoning.[143] On the other hand, if the rezoning will create a traffic hazard it should be rejected.[144]

The adequacy of the highway system as a factor in rezoning raises the question whether the nature of the highway system should influence land use policy or whether the priorities should be the other way around. When a new highway has actually been built, or is proposed, the court is apparently willing to accept it as a factor favorable to rezoning. Since the absence of highway facilities is counted against the rezoning,

---

[142] Strine, *The Use of Conditions in Land-Use Control,* 67 Dick. L. Rev. 109 (1963).

[143] Marcus v. Montgomery County Council, 235 Md. 535, 201 A.2d 777 (1964).

[144] Kramer v. Board of County Comm'rs, 248 Md. 27, 234 A.2d 589 (1967); Tauber v. Montgomery County Council, 244 Md. 332, 223 A.2d 615 (1966).

the only conclusion is that the zoning authorities have been asked to defer to the highway planners when it comes to allocating land uses. Given the importance of accessibility as a factor in apartment location, this attitude of the court may require the zoning agencies to give away their control over a significant input to the land development process. Yet consider the court's approval, in a floating zone case, of a neighborhood rezone which called for the integration of multi-family with commercial development.[145] Here the court was impressed by the influence of the development on trip patterns, pointing out that trips would be reduced by placing employment centers near apartment development. But the point might be made that trip patterns would have been considered when the highway network was planned. Density increases permitted by the zoning authorities can upset the highway planners' projections, and might even impair the adequacy of the highway system in the long run. We will review one attempt to coordinate highway planning and zoning policy in our Seattle study.

8. Improved water and sewer facilities justify apartment development,[146] and a lack of either is a reason for denying an apartment rezone.[147] Again, this attitude leaves the local water and sewer authorities with a major influence over new development. There was evidence of an indiscriminate extension of sewer and water facilities in the suburban areas of Washington,[148] and these policies would also do much to foreclose the options that were open to the zoning agencies.


*Judicial Response: The Development Sequence*


What is lacking from cases like those decided in Maryland is any sense of the sequence of development as it is affected by an

---

[145] Bigenho v. Montgomery County Council, 248 Md. 386, 237 A.2d 53 (1968).

[146] Meginniss v. Trustees of the Sheppard and Enoch Pratt Hosp., 246 Md. 704, 229 A.2d 417 (1967); Finney v. Halle, 241 Md. 224, 216 A.2d 530 (1966).

[147] Gorin v. Board of County Comm'rs, 244 Md. 106, 223 A.2d 237 (1966).

[148] G.M. Neutze, The Suburban Apartment Boom 49-50 (1968).

accumulation of zoning decisions over a period of time. Even with the heavy litigation of apartment zoning in the Maryland appellate court, the decided cases represent a tiny fraction of all the apartment developments in any area over any period of time. More cases would have been litigated at the trial court level and not appealed, but even these can be expected to be few in number as compared with the total caseload. In three cases, however, the Maryland Court of Appeals considered over a short time span a series of appeals in apartment rezonings adjacent to a heavily travelled thoroughfare leading out of the District of Columbia. Map 2 locates the zoning sites in these three decisions. The cases are important to our inquiry because a master plan covering this part of the county had been adopted just three years before the first case was decided, and was in effect throughout the entire sequence.

In the first of these cases, *Marcus v. Montgomery County Council*,[149] decided in 1964, four rezoning applications were combined for appeal. Two of these were multi-family, one was commercial, and one was for office development. Original zoning in 1928 placed these properties in a single family residential category, this zoning was confirmed by a comprehensive rezoning in 1954, and again by a land use plan adopted for this part of the county in 1961. Nevertheless, since the last zoning ordinance, and indeed since adoption of the plan, substantial changes had occurred in the area, including the construction of a shopping center adjoining one of the properties, and the construction of apartments within "easy sight" of the parcels for which rezoning was asked. However, we are not told the size of the shopping center or the apartment development, nor are we told how these developments arrived at this location. Were they contemplated by the plan and ordinance, or did they come there as the consequence of amendments, floating zones or similar procedures?

The court had to consider first the effect of the comprehensive plan on the zoning ordinance and the requested amendments. In an elaboration of principles discussed earlier, the court noted that the adoption of the plan without change in the

---

[149] 235 Md. 535, 201 A.2d 777 (1964). This case had political overtures which do not appear in the court's opinion, as it was one of a series of rezones granted at the same time by an outgoing council.

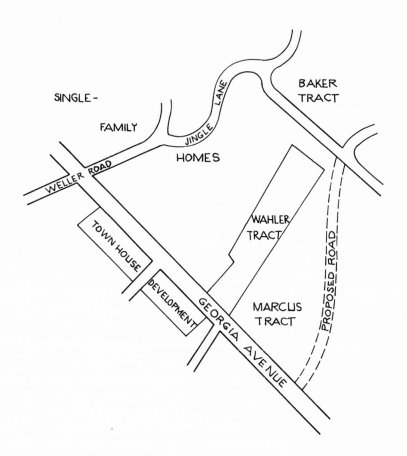

MAP 2: MONTGOMERY COUNTY, MARYLAND:
ZONING SITES.

zoning was "entitled to the presumption that it was a deliberate confirmation of the earlier [zoning] decision."[150] Nevertheless, the court felt entitled to consider changes in the environment which had occurred, not only since the plan, but subsequent to the original zoning and prior to the adoption of the plan. In the face of objections from the planning staff and a 3-2 negative vote by the planning commission, the county council had granted the rezones. With little discussion, the court affirmed under the fairly debatable rule. So be it. From one perspective the decision upholding the rezoning is anti-planning, since the plan was not followed and the plan commission overruled. How consistent the court's and the council's decision is with the zoning criteria we have elaborated from the pattern of Maryland court decisions is another matter. At least the presence of adjacent intensive development would suggest that the area had become committed to a more intensive development pattern than the plan contemplated. The opinion leaves us dissatisfied.

In any event, a rezoning in the same area was to come again before the Court of Appeals not fifteen months later. *Baker v. Montgomery County Council*[151] considered the rezoning by the council of a thirty-acre tract abutting one of the parcels in the *Marcus* case which had been zoned multi-family. Now we are told that the tract rezoned to apartments in *Marcus* contained 27 acres, and that the commercial and apartment rezonings previous to the *Marcus* case were very small. They are to the south of the tract which came before the court in *Baker*. Again, in *Baker*, staff and planning commission recommended against the rezoning, but council approved. In *Baker*, however, the court invalidated the rezoning and ignored the fairly debatable rule which so firmly reinforced the *Marcus* decision. In a brief reference to the *Marcus* case, the court held that apartment rezoning to create a buffer zone, as in that case, "does not always warrant the rezoning of adjacent property."[152] Inspection of the *Marcus* opinion indicates, however, that the court did not rely on the buffer concept. Nonetheless, reliance on the buffer concept was found to be implicit in *Marcus*, the *Baker* decision

---

[150] Marcus v. Montgomery County Council, 235 Md. 535, 539, 540, 201 A.2d 777, 780 (1964).

[151] 241 Md. 178, 215 A.2d 831 (1966).

[152] *Id.* at 185, 215 A.2d at 835.

relying on the reasons for the rezoning in *Marcus* which had been given by the *county council.*

The area next came to the attention of the appellate court in a rezoning to apartment development of a five-acre tract which was considered in *Wahler v. Montgomery County Council,* early in 1968.[153] The tract in *Wahler* was adjacent to the *Marcus* tract, on which rezoning had been granted, and the *Baker* tract, on which rezoning had been denied. On the same day the *Wahler* tract was rezoned to multi-family, a four-acre tract adjacent to the northwest was zoned to townhouse development under a floating zone procedure. By this time the planning staff had changed its mind on the future of this area. Noting that the *Wahler* tract was "surrounded" by multi-family use, it recommended the rezoning. The planning commission concurred and the council approvingly rezoned. By the time of the council decision, however, the Maryland Court of Appeals had decided the *Baker* case, in which it had invalidated the *Baker* rezoning.

Again, the Court of Appeals reversed. While there is more in the opinion than comment on land use, the highest appellate court once more invoked the buffer extension rule of *Baker.* Approval of the buffering apartment rezone in *Marcus* was not intended as blanket approval of indefinite extensions of buffers in the immediate area. Also stressed was the fact that by the time of the council's decision on the *Wahler* application, the rezoning in the *Baker* case had been reversed.

Emphasis on the court's reversal of the rezoning in *Baker* also weakened the reasoning of planning staff that the *Wahler* tract was "surrounded" by multi-family uses. But the court still had to deal with the townhouse zoning which had been approved on the same day as the *Wahler* rezoning, and which was not before the court simply because it had not been appealed. The court had no difficulty on this score. The townhouse zone was granted as part of a floating zone process. "Accord and harmony with the surrounding zoning are essential to its validity."[154] Therefore, approval of the townhouse zoning was not a change in the character of the neighborhood. But the court was

---

[153] 249 Md. 62, 238 A.2d 266 (1968).

[154] *Id.* at 68, 238 A.2d at 269.

hard put to defend itself. Whatever the process by which the townhouse development was allowed, it can be argued that the townhouse development is closely akin to a multi-family use. The court was aware of this problem:

> It cannot be said, of course, that the creation of the R-T [townhouse] zone did not effect some change. Whatever change did take place, however, must be assumed, absent persuasive evidence to the contrary, to have been compatible with the residential character of the neighborhood.[155]

There was a dissenting opinion which in part took exception with the court's evaluation of the floating zone basis of the townhouse approval.

Whatever can be said about this sequence of cases, it is clear that the court's continuing involvement in rezonings in the area forced it more and more to a consideration of the substance of the planning process. Note that in two of the three cases it reversed a council rezoning in the face of its own fairly debatable rule. Note also that the court was increasingly pressed to substitute its own conception of land development in the area for the conception entertained in the master plan and, ultimately, by the planning staff itself. What has happened, of course, is that the lack of direction for these zoning decisions forced the highest judicial body of the state into a series of ad hoc decisions on applications for apartment development in the area. These uncertainties were aggravated by the master plan, which showed the entire area surrounding these three rezone sites for single family uses. No apartments were contemplated, and once introduced in the first rezoning they were hard to handle as subsequent apartment applications came up for consideration. These so-called "Jingle Lane" controversies (see the map) are locally famous, and the fact that the first rezoning was one of a series carried out by a lame duck county council simply underscores the political risks that inhere in the planning and zoning process.

---

[155] *Id.* at 69, 238 A.2d at 270.

Perhaps because the land use plan did not speak to the apartment question, the court fell back in these three cases on its assessment of neighborhood externalities; thus its disapproval of the extension of buffers. But what was the "planning" basis for this position? From the neighborhood perspective, the discrimination complaint is persuasive; it was raised by the developer in the *Baker* litigation. We could fall back on the presumption of constitutionality and allow the local legislative body to make these decisions, but the Maryland court was unwilling to do this after its first decision. We might also fall back on our earlier position that it is the function of the plan to make these tradeoffs, but if we do then we must find some basis in law for implementing these community land use decisions in a neighborhood context in which they may seem arbitrary.

The problem is raised by another pair of Maryland cases, *Bigenho v. Montgomery County Council*, [156] and *Brown v. Wimpress*, [157] decided in 1967 and 1968. At issue was the development at an interchange of two major limited-access highways. A 1957 land use plan had designated each of the quadrants of the interchange as a separate planning area. The southwest quadrant was already developed as a country club with adjacent rural residential housing. The northwest quadrant was designated by the plan as a shopping center. Both the northeast and southeast quadrants were zoned single family residential, but the plan included a "symbol" in the northeast quadrant which indicated that it was a potential site for an employment center. (Remember that the local land use plans were at this time quite detailed.)

*Bigenho* considered the rezoning of a 270-acre tract which occupied the northeast quadrant. In a rezoning which was partly conventional and partly based on the floating zone process, the county council approved a package of rezones which contemplated the development of an integrated commercial, industrial, and multi-family complex. This rezoning the court finally approved, relying in part on the plan's symbolic designation of the employment center potential, and noting as well that construction of apartments in the vicinity of the commercial and

---

[156] 248 Md. 386, 237 A.2d 53 (1968).
[157] 250 Md. 200, 242 A.2d 157 (1968).

industrial development would provide accommodation for those living in the immediate area and reduce outgoing and incoming trips. Complementary use patterns were important in the *Bigenho* case.

They did not count in *Brown v. Wimpress*, in which the court reversed the multi-family rezoning of a 38-acre tract in the southeast quadrant of the same interchange, which occurred after *Bigenho*. In part, the court relied in *Brown* on the decision in the master plan to use major highways as dividing lines for planning purposes between the four quadrants, on the fact that the rest of the southeast quadrant had been developed as zoned for single-family residences, on some evidence of political skull-duggery in the rezone, and (arguably by quoting *Bigenho*) on the point that the size of the *Bigenho* tract justified its treatment for zoning purpose without regard to externalities. The rule against extension of buffers was also cited. The *Bigenho-Brown* sequence shows more attention to the master plan, and it can be argued that the plan in these cases was more useful as a guide to potential development patterns. Nevertheless, the court might have been better off relying on the role of the plan as a tradeoff of development possibilities at the community level, rather than justifying on the basis of neighborhood external-ities. A convincing dissent in *Brown* argued that the external-ities created by the extensive development in *Bigenho* had an effect on land development in the southwest quadrant, and should have been considered in the *Brown* litigation.

## Conclusion

We began this chapter with an analysis of the role of the plan in the zoning process, and with the zoning techniques through which the proposals of the comprehensive plan could be implemented by the zoning system. We saw that the manage-ment of change in the urban environment was one of the most pressing problems in zoning control, but that the standard zon-ing act had failed to give it sufficient attention. Especially in urbanizing areas, zoning authorities may pursue a policy of watchful waiting. They put aside any meaningful advance zon-ing, and rely for their zoning policy on zoning changes which are made in response to applications from individual developers. These changes may be made by a variety of techniques, ranging all the way from use variances, through conditional uses and exceptions, to the simple zoning amendment. We concentrated on the zoning amendment as the purest form of legislative change, and one which was explicitly related by statute to the guidelines of the comprehensive plan.

We next turned to the judicial reception of the comprehensive planning process, and its influence through zoning, and we found a good deal of confusion and some distrust of legislative amendment techniques to carry out zoning change. Constitutional presumptions supporting the validity of local legislative action jostled with distrust of zoning changes initiated by individual developers to produce cases like *Roseta*. Here the court shifted the presumption and showed disfavor with the legislative change even though it was arguably in accord with the proposals of the comprehensive plan. For a closer look at the judicial reception of planning and zoning judgments we turned next to a series of Maryland appellate court cases. These cases considered zoning amendments for apartments in suburban sections of Baltimore and Washington, where there had been a high level of planning activity. We found that the comprehensive plan was simply one element in the court's handling of apartment zoning. Partly impressed by the fact that the plan operates on a more distant time horizon, partly committed to a point of view which accords the plan an advisory role, the Maryland court was more attentive to physical change in the immediate environment of an apartment rezone than it was to the proposals of the plan. If there is any lasting impression from the Maryland cases, it is that the dynamics of development in fast-growing areas soon outruns both the plan and the zoning ordinance, leaving the court with the need to exercise a judgment which must often be ad hoc.

One other important limitation on judicial involvement with the planning and zoning process, especially at the appellate level, must be noted. Court attention to the zoning problems of any one area is episodic, at best. Where, as in Maryland, the court is forced into a closer examination of zoning policy in a series of cases arising from the same area, it has increasingly usurped the planning function from the local agencies, contrary to its dictates on the presumption of constitutionality to be accorded the local legislative judgment. Judicial zoning at this scale is hardly to be welcomed. But what do we find when we examine the zoning record of a local zoning agency as it deals, over time, with its workload of zoning controversies? Does zoning policy, which is viewed by the courts through the diluted perspective mandated by its review function, gain more content when it is applied from case to case by local zoning authorities which face no such limitations? Does the role of the comprehensive plan gain more meaning as we view its implementation in the daily workload of zoning administration? For answers to questions like these we turn to an examination of zoning administration in a rapidly-growing urban area in the Pacific Northwest. And we concentrate once more on our problem of apartment development in suburban areas.

## ZONING IN SUBURBIA: AN APARTMENT
## POLICY FOR SEATTLE'S SUBURBS

We turn now to an examination in practice of the planning and zoning system which we have described in the preceding pages. The setting for our study is the Seattle, Washington, metropolitan area, and more especially King County, the urbanizing county in which the city of Seattle is located. The subject of our study is the apartment zoning problem which has been the focus of our concern in our analysis of the planning and zoning process.

Like many other suburban areas, King County outside Seattle has experienced an apartment boom. Informally, the planning department indicates that multiple units increased from a total of eight per cent of all housing starts in 1960-61 to over fifty per cent of all starts in 1967. This development has not been unguided by the planning process. In 1964 the county adopted a comprehensive plan of the policy statement variety. The plan called for a development policy which encouraged centers of urban concentration, and apartments were seen as a vital ingredient in the development of these centers. To implement its policies, moreover, the King County plan contained a series of guidelines on various types of development, including apartments, and apartment development had almost always followed legislative zoning amendments which had been processed by the zoning agencies under the guidelines of the comprehensive plan. Given this legal and planning setting, King County presented an excellent opportunity to test both the impact of a comprehensive plan on the zoning process, and the role that zoning played in the regulation and control of development. We will examine the role of the plan and the zoning process through a computer analysis of 170 apartment rezoning applications, which were processed by the King County zoning agencies during this period of intensified apartment activity. Our

purpose is to consider this zoning record in light of the theories
we have developed so far concerning the role and function of
the planning system, and the substantive principles which control the decision on apartment rezones.

### The Zoning and Planning Framework in King County

Dry words in a text should not hide the magic of the Puget
Sound area. Framed by the waters of the Sound, by the Olympic Peninsula with its Olympic Range to the west, by the Cas-
cade Range some forty miles to the east, and blessed with lakes
and a dazzling setting of hills and valleys, Seattle and the Puget
Sound region have always been a natural wonderland. By the
close of the 1960's the area was rapidly urbanizing and could
claim nearly two million people in the basin which stretched
from Vancouver, Canada, on the north, to Olympia, the state
capital and a city of 21,000 at the base of the Sound, on the
south.

Unfortunately, the planning problems of the region have
been complicated by its political division into a tier of rectan-
gular counties, running east and west on their longest boundaries, and slicing into the urbanized portions of the area along
boundary lines which are senseless from a planning perspective.
King County illustrates the point. It is large, as are many western counties—approximately 2,200 square miles in size—and so
it covers a large part of the urbanizing sector of the Seattle
metropolitan area. On the eve of our study, as Table 1 indicates,
the unincorporated sections of King County under the zoning
jurisdiction of the county government contained about three-
fourths of the county population outside Seattle, so that county zoning covered a significant portion of the county's area.
Even so, topographic features and the pattern of existing incorporations combined to create an incongruous county zoning
jurisdiction of urban leftovers, large areas undergoing urbanization, and uninhabitable mountains and upland. Some basic geo-
graphy will help here. Based on Puget Sound, the urban and
urbanizing western segments of King County are divided by two
oblong fresh water lakes, running north and south, into two
parallel land corridors. The corridor to the west, bordered by

the Sound and Lake Washington, is occupied by the City of Seattle. Between Lake Washington and the smaller Lake Sammamish is an interlake corridor occupied by several incorporated suburban municipalities. In addition to the interlake municipalities, several older and more stable suburbs lie in the valley to the south of Lake Washington. King County also retained jurisdiction of urban patches to the north and south of Seattle which the city had been unwilling to annex. Map 3 indicates the extent of incorporation in King County at the time of this study. As the map shows, King County was typical of most American urban counties in its combination of leftover, unincorporated urban segments, and larger, vaster areas in which urbanization was just beginning.

## TABLE 1.  ESTIMATED POPULATION IN SEATTLE-KING COUNTY, APRIL, 1968

| | |
|---|---|
| Seattle .................... | 587,000 |
| King County, unincorporated ..... | 436,600 |
| King County municipalities ...... | 166,400 |
| TOTAL | 1,190,000 |

Source: King County Department of Planning

After this study was finished, King County reorganized under a new charter which eliminated the conventional planning commission and revamped the zoning process, but these changes only consolidate and somewhat modify the more conventional zoning system which was in operation at the time this study took place. King County was then governed by a three-man Board of County Commissioners, and conducted its planning and zoning activities with a conventional, nine-member planning commission and a planning staff headed by an appointed planning director.

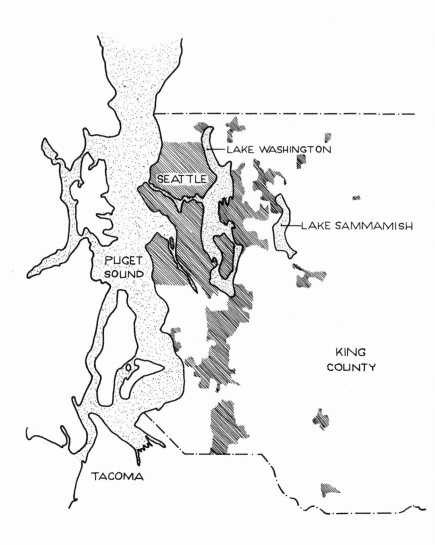

MAP 3: MAJOR INCORPORATED AREAS
OF KING COUNTY AS OF 1968.

As a legal basis for the conduct of the planning and zoning function, the state statutes provided an optional legislative framework which King County had decided to utilize, and which departs in significant detail from the standard planning and zoning acts we analyzed previously. Most important to us is the much stronger relationship between the plan and the zoning ordinance which the Washington statute contemplates. This relationship first becomes apparent in the statutory definition of the comprehensive plan:

> [T]he policies and proposals approved and recommended by the planning agency or initiated by the board [of county commissioners] and approved by motion of the board (a) as a beginning step in planning for the physical development of the county; (b) as the means for coordinating county programs and services; (c) as a source of reference to aid in developing, correlating, and coordinating official regulations and controls; and (d) as a means for promoting the general welfare.[158]

Land use and circulation "elements" are required of all plans,[159] while other components are optional, including housing, transportation, and urban renewal elements.[160]

To implement the comprehensive plan, the Washington statute authorizes what are called "official controls"[161] and which clearly contemplate a zoning ordinance. Again departing from the more ambiguous language of the Standard Act, the Washington statute requires a land use plan containing at least the mandatory land use and circulation elements before "Zoning maps as an official control may be adopted. . . ."[162]

We must now look at how the zoning system in King County was utilized to authorize apartment developments, and we

---

[158] Wash. Rev. Code § 36.70.020(6) (1964).

[159] *Id.* § 36.70.550, 36.70.560.

[160] *Id.* § 36.70.350.

[161] *Id.* §§ 36.70.550, 36.70.560.

[162] *Id.* § 36.70.720.

have already noted that apartments were handled through amendments to the zoning ordinance. Neither of our alternative methods—the conditional use or the use variance—were utilized for apartment development during the period of our study. This was so even though the statute authorized both the conditional use and the use variance. The statute created a conventional zoning board of adjustment, and this board has the statutory power to grant conditional uses[163] "as provided by the ordinance." But an inspection of the King County Zoning Code indicates that apartments were not treated under the conditional use procedure. The statutory section creating the board of adjustment also authorizes zoning variances; there is no limitation on the granting of variances in use, and the language of the King County Zoning Code likewise contains no explicit limitation on use variances.[164] However, the policy in the county had been to handle changes in use through the amendment procedure, and the board of adjustment had not been granting use variances, at least for apartments.

We return, therefore, to the zoning amendment as the available procedure to make land use changes which can include apartment development. The statute provides a procedure for amending official controls, including the zoning ordinance. This procedure is somewhat inexplicit, but it does contemplate a series of approvals for zoning amendments, ending in an approval by the county board.[165] The process starts with a recommendation by the planning commission following a public hearing, the commission to state the "findings of fact . . . and the reasons for its action. . . ."[166] All amendments must then be approved by the board of county commissioners, which does not have to hold a public hearing unless it wishes to make a "change" in the commission's recommendations.[167] If a hearing

---

[163] *Id.* § 36.70.810. *Cf.* State *ex rel.* Kadow v. Board of Adjustment of City of Vancouver, 464 P.2d 418 (Wash. 1970) (Conditional use for apartments properly granted).

[164] King County Zoning Code § 24.58.020 [hereinafter cited as Zoning Code].

[165] Wash. Rev. Code §§ 36.70.570—36.70.660 (1964).

[166] *Id.* § 36.70.600.

[167] *Id.* § 36.70.630.

is held, the board must "adopt its own findings of fact and statement setting forth the factors considered at the hearing and its own analysis of findings considered by it to be controlling."[168]

This rudimentary procedure was expanded by the county zoning ordinance, and the provisions of the ordinance had in turn been qualified in practice. For one thing, the statute did not indicate how the amendment process was to be initiated. This omission was remedied by the ordinance, which authorized owners of property to file amendment applications.[169] In practice, almost all zoning amendments for apartments were initiated this way. A hearing by the planning commission was also required by the ordinance, and in practice the planning department conducted an *ex parte* investigation of an owner's proposed amendment and filed a report containing its recommendations with the commission before the commission hearing was held. This report was at no time made available to the applicant. If the amendment was approved by the commission, the ordinance required that it be sent to the board of county commissioners, which was instructed to hold a public hearing.[170] The ordinance also provided that appeals to the board could be taken by the applicant from a planning commission denial, and by "any aggrieved person" from a planning commission approval.[171] In practice, the board passed formally on all recommendations for approval which were forwarded by the commission but held hearings only on appeals, even though the ordinance was silent on whether a hearing on an appeal was required. The ordinance was also conflicting on what reports were to be forwarded to the board for its consideration. In the case of a planning commission approval, apparently without an appeal, the findings of the commission were to be forwarded to the board. If there was an appeal the planning department was to file a report with the board, apparently indicating the basis on which the planning commission's decision was made.[172] In prac-

---

[168] *Id.*

[169] Zoning Code § 24.60.030.

[170] *Id.* § 24.60.040.

[171] *Id.* § 24.60.100.

[172] *Id.* § 24.60.110.

tice, the entire zoning file went to the board, containing both the planning department's initial recommendation and the planning commission's findings.

To summarize, then, the zoning amendment procedure in King County worked about as follows:

1. The owner of the land made application for an amendment.

2. The planning department staff reviewed the application and made a report *ex parte* to the planning commission.

3. The planning commission held a hearing and decided whether to approve, deny, or modify the application.

4. The planning commission decision stood unless there was an appeal, either by the applicant from a denial or by an "aggrieved" party, usually a neighbor or groups of neighbors, from an approval.

5. The board of county commissioners held hearings on all appeals, and reached a decision either affirming, reversing, or modifying the action of the planning commission. In practice, the board hearing was *de novo* to the extent that it took new evidence and reached its own conclusion on the information presented, including the report of the department. The scope of the board hearing was limited, however, by an informal understanding that if the applicant substantially shifted his ground the case would be sent back to the planning commission for additional review. Another limitation on the board's powers was another understanding, also informal, that the board would not reverse if both the planning department and the planning commission concurred in the recommendation, whether favorable or not.

We have then, as a consequence of statutory and ordinance provision, and as modified by practice, a hybrid administrative and legislative process very similar to the procedure approved by the highest New York court in the *Tarrytown* case. We can simplify our inquiry by characterizing the planning department function as an initial though *ex parte* determination on the application, the planning commission and board providing an intermediate and final review subject to the qualification that each agency took evidence and heard the application anew. The hearings that were conducted were informal and were not adjudicative in the strict sense. While a transcript of the actual proceedings was not made, the amendment process produced a comparatively rich data file for each case and was preserved in the zoning records.

We might now consider the pattern of supreme court zoning decisions in the State of Washington as it had developed up to the time of the study. We have some guidance to the court's attitude toward the role of the comprehensive plan in the zoning process, but not much. The court has considered whether adoption of the comprehensive plan is essential to the validity of the zoning ordinance, and has decided in the context of the municipal zoning statutes that it is not, and has adopted the conventional view that the plan can be expressed in the ordinance.[173] Some legislative rezoning cases have recently been decided, the supreme court handling them under the "spot" zoning rubric. While the court does not appear limited by the Maryland change-mistake rule, it has been opposed to isolated rezonings on small tracts for commercial uses or high-rise apartments in single family areas. On the other hand, it approved the extension of an existing business zone to permit the construction of a large shopping center on a 53-acre tract in King County. In the last case, the court was impressed with the fact that the zoning was merely an extension of an existing business zone—our external economy problem. Otherwise, the court's attitude toward rezonings on small tracts is typical. One of these spot zoning cases would have allowed a filling station to be constructed in a single family residential area in King County. The case arose after the adoption of the King County policies plan, and the court relied on the policies of the plan for business development in rejecting the rezoning in an isolated area in which business zoning of this type was disfavored by the plan. This case at least gives implicit support to reliance on the plan in making legislative amendments to the zoning ordinance which authorize changes in use, although the supreme court has not yet relied on the plan to uphold rather than reject a zoning amendment. The cases are collected in the footnote.[174] We

---

[173] Shelton v. City of Bellevue, 73 Wash. 2d 28, 435 P.2d 949 (1968).

[174] The cases rejecting spot rezones in residential areas are Anderson v. City of Seattle, 64 Wash. 2d 198, 390 P.2d 994 (1964) (high-rise apartment); Pierce v. King County, 62 Wash. 2d 324, 382 P.2d 628 (1963). (filling station). The shopping center case is McNaughton v. Boeing, 68

might also note that none of the apartment rezoning cases in our study were appealed to the trial court, much less the supreme court.

In summary, we find no limitation on the zoning agencies in King County other than implicit judicial approval of the plan as a guide to the zoning process, and judicial disfavor of small "spot" zones in residential areas. With this background in mind, we look next at the King County comprehensive plan, and at the detailed structure of the zoning ordinance under which the apartment rezone cases were decided.

## The King County Comprehensive Plan [175] and Zoning Ordinance

We noted earlier the difference between more conventional comprehensive land use plans which contain maps of land use proposals, and a plan like the one adopted by King County, which may or may not contain a map but which relies extensively on written planning policies. The King County plan does contain a map, but the scale is too large to reflect adequately the plan's proposals, and the plan relies heavily on its written policy statements. Since we focus on apartments, we will concentrate on the policies proposed in the King County plan for the residential growth of the county, and on the contribution which apartments were to make to that growth. The plan begins, as do many plans, with a regional frame of reference, by considering all of the area of King County, including Seattle and the incorporated municipalities. This decision was justified by legal authority to do planning for the entire county, even though implementary zoning authority was limited to unincor-

---

Wash. 2d 659, 414 P.2d 778 (1966). *See also* Smith v. Skagit County 453 P.2d 832 (Wash. 1969); Farrell v. City of Seattle, 452 P.2d 965 (Wash. 1969); Carlson v. City of Bellevue, 73 Wash. 2d 41, 435 P.2d 957 (1968). For an earlier discussion of the Washington zoning cases see Morris, *Toward Effective Municipal Zoning*, 35 Wash. L. Rev. 534 (1960).

[175] King County Planning Dep't, The Comprehensive Plan for King County, Washington (June 23, 1964) [hereinafter cited as Plan]. The King County plan is discussed in F.H. Beal, *Defining Development Objectives*, in W.I. Goodman & E.C. Freund; Principles and Practice of Urban Planning 327, 342-43 (1968).

porated areas.[176] After discussing centralization and dispersal alternatives as two extreme models for the county's growth, the plan settles on an urban center development concept as a compromise.[177] Why this alternative is picked is explained only in general terms—to increase living choice, to preserve natural beauty, to separate major portions of the urban area—but the urban center policy is accompanied by a diagrammatic map which locates potential urban center development points, although it is not clear whether the map is supposed to be illustrative or definitive. These proposals are presented in Map 4, which is derived from the plan's presentation of the urban center development concept. Informally, the planning department has indicated that the location of potential urban centers was supposed to be at least *prima facie* binding. This interpretation is supported by a reference to the official comprehensive plan map which accompanies the comprehensive plan, as the high density residential centers located on the official map correspond somewhat to the urban centers located on Map 4. But the official plan map is difficult to read, and the correspondence is approximate. What criteria should be used to locate the urban centers are not specified, moreover, although the plan does state that "Most of the Urban Centers would be expansions of existing development."[178]

We find more explicit policies for land use arrangements within urban centers, and with reference to our apartment problem the plan does state that "In general, high-density housing types would be encouraged to develop relatively close to Urban Centers . . . in order that traffic volume generated by these densities would be adjacent to their service facilities."[179] The plan goes on to say that these density objectives can be achieved by "encouraging" apartment development as well as single family homes at urban center points. In addition, the plan recognizes that the transportation system should provide the framework for implementing the urban center development concept.[180] A

[176] Plan at v; Wash. Rev. Code § 36.70.320 (1964).

[177] Plan at 26, 27.

[178] Plan at 29.

[179] *Id.*

[180] Plan at 30.

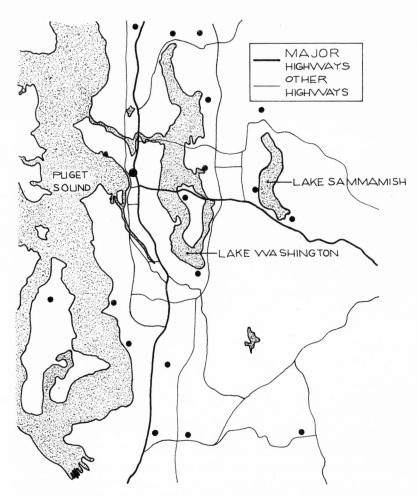

MAP 4: URBAN CENTER DEVELOPMENT CONCEPT.

reference to Map 4 will indicate that the transportation system in the King County region is shaped by two major traffic arteries along north-south and east-west corridors. These intersect in Seattle, and are complemented by a radial system of supplementary major highways. Given this framework, we would expect the implementation of the urban centers concept, as the King County planners saw it, to produce a series of scattered high-intensity development based on the highway network, most probably at major highway intersections. Just exactly this kind of local development pattern appears contemplated by Figure 2-11 of the plan, reproduced as Map 5.[181]

To summarize, the King County plan contemplated a series of high-intensity development centers positioned on major highway intersections and characterized in part by high density apartment uses. This developmental model fits very well with the taste hierarchies in residential use which we have observed before, and which see apartments as filling a buffer role. In the King County plan, however, this buffer role was toned down, though not ignored. Grouping apartments near major highways was favored primarily as a method of creating desirable activity patterns, as the planners wanted to complement high density residential development with business and other activity centers to reduce work trips, although there is no explicit recognition of the traffic congestion problem that appeared in the Maryland cases. We have already noticed that the Maryland appellate court was willing to validate this planning concept as the basis for its decision in the *Bigenho* case. Zoning policies for apartments in King County were therefore a mixture of community-wide decisions which considered the most optimum structure for area-wide development, and locally-related spatial policies which were attentive to land use relationships on the more limited neighborhood scale.

These ideas are evident in the more detailed policies for apartments which appear later in the plan, and which are reproduced in Figure 1.[182] The apartment zoning policies are difficult to summarize easily. For one thing, they contemplate slightly different criteria for high density as distinguished from

---

[181] *See* Plan at 33.

[182] *See* Plan at 117-19.

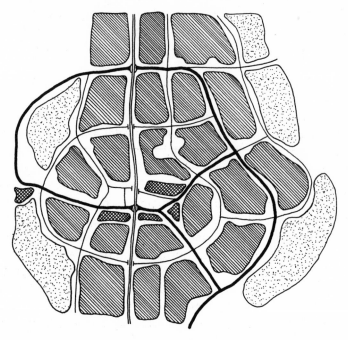

■ HIGH DENSITY ▨ MEDIUM DENSITY ▨ LOW DENSITY

MAP 5: RESIDENTIAL DENSITIES AT URBAN CENTERS.

## FIGURE 1. APARTMENT DEVELOPMENT POLICIES IN THE KING COUNTY COMPREHENSIVE PLAN

*Multi-Family Residential Areas*

Multi-family residential development generally consists of a number of housing units contained within one structure. They may range from two units in a structure to any number depending on the size parcel of land, or they may range in densities up to a maximum of 36 housing units per gross acre.

Because their high densities create a concentrated demand within a given geographic area, their locations must be interrelated with the circulation system and other land uses. Multi-family residential areas may be allowed only in locations which meet the following criteria:

> Multi-family residential areas shall *always* be located functionally convenient to a major or secondary arterial highway. Adequate arterial and collector streets should exist prior to or be developed concurrently with the establishment of such uses.

> Since multi-family residential areas are complementary to shopping areas and other primary service facilities, they may logically be developed adjacent to such uses.

> In order that a maximum number of persons can take advantage of the amenities of view, water access, and permanent open space, multi-family residential use may be located in or adjacent to such areas, provided that multistory structures are so located and designed as to not destroy such amenities for adjoining existing or potential residential areas.

While apartments may be compatible with certain commercial uses, multi-family residential development requires the same protection as single family development from obnoxious uses. A multi-family residential area, therefore, is not per se a proper buffer or transition between single family residential and manufacturing or other incompatible land use areas.

In addition to providing a variety of housing types, multi-family residences provide living areas for the maximum number of persons in proximity to and with convenient access to the services and facilities of trade, cultural and employment centers. Further, multiples located in proximity to these centers minimize traffic congestion created by the movement of large numbers of persons.

Applying these principles to the URBAN CENTER DEVELOPMENT concept, the higher densities of multi-family residences should be located near the larger trade or employment centers.

> The high densities of multiple residential use shall be located adjoining or convenient to major highways with preference given to those routes which provide the most convenient and direct access (in terms of travel time) to the major trade and employment centers of the area.

> The high densities of multiple residential use should be located adjoining either major shopping areas, cultural centers (at urban or multi-community level), or locations having special amenities of view, water access, or permanent open space.

> The lower densities of multiple residential use shall be located adjoining or convenient to major *or* secondary arterial streets.

> The lower densities of multiple residential use should be located adjoining either business areas, cultural or community centers, or locations having special amenities of view, water access, or permanent open space.

> The lower densities of multiple residential use may be located as a transitional use between higher density multiples and single family residential densities.

low density apartment developments. In practice, this distinction has not been applied, as apartment development at the highest densities contemplated by the plan has not been carried out. As the highest apartment densities require high-rise structures, these are subject to more stringent building code requirements which push building costs beyond the point of economic feasibility. As a result, planning department studies show that at least on tracts of five acres or more, apartment densities in actual developments average twenty units to the acre. In appraising the effectiveness of the plan as a guide to the zoning process, therefore, we will drop the plan's distinctions between high density and low density apartments.

We must next add that apartment rezone applications close to high amenity locations, or to cultural and manufacturing centers, did not appear in our sample. As a consequence, we are left with those criteria in the plan which call for apartment rezoning in the vicinity of arterials, and of business centers. While the plan is not entirely clear, location near an arterial appears essential, while location near a business center is strongly preferred. In short, the policies of the plan simply articulate in writing the assumptions underlying the neighborhood development model reproduced in Map 5, which is taken from the plan.

We can turn next to the more specific regulations of the zoning ordinance to see how the more general policies of the comprehensive plan were implemented in the zoning process. Before we do so an additional word about highway planning in the Seattle area would seem to be in order, in view of the importance of the transportation network to planning and zoning policy. At the time the King County plan was adopted a regional transportation study was underway in the Puget Sound area which was to publish its report three years later, in 1967. A highway plan was also published in 1967 as part of the King County plan, and it was this plan which served as the basis for implementing the King County urban centers concept. The point to make is that there are differences between the King County highway plan and the regional transportation plan which have an important impact on zoning policy. In particular, the regional plan showed a new freeway running north and south in the corridor between the two lakes—the so-called Lake

Hills Expressway—which was not included in the King County highway plan. While expressways are excluded as location points for apartment development in the King County comprehensive plan because they do not provide direct access, a new expressway would nonetheless appear to have an important impact on the distribution of the development centers that were chosen. For example, arterials feeding the expressway would be prime sites for apartment and urban center development. Failure to take account of the regional highway plan is especially important in view of a decision, apparently made by the state highway department in 1968, to give the Lake Hills Expressway an urgent priority. This lack of coordination simply illustrates the oft-made point about fragmentation of power in metropolitan regions. The point should also be made that the policy orientation of the King County plan would easily have permitted consideration of the Lake Hills route, since King County zoning agencies could have based their zoning decisions on that highway proposal without having to change the official plan map. That they chose not to do so is all the more interesting in view of the controversy that the Lake Hills route later engendered. But this is another story.

Let us now turn to the King County zoning ordinance. A preliminary point to make is that the King County ordinance was in the process of revision at the time of this study. A "new" zoning code had recently been adopted, and it was gradually replacing the "old" zoning code throughout the county. By the time of the study, the new code had been adopted throughout most of the urbanizing area, although the "old" code still applied in the more remote sections and some "old" code cases are included in the study sample. In the discussion that follows, reference will be made to the new code; apart from some innovations to be discussed, the new code differs from the old primarily in the more simplified framework which is provided for residential development.

Figure 2 shows the residential zoning designations contained in the King County code, and the uses and densities permitted within each classification. In addition, there were three business zones, three industrial zones, and a classification for quarrying and mining. As zoning ordinances go, the King County classifications are comparatively simple. We should first note that the

# FIGURE 2. ZONING CLASSIFICATIONS IN KING COUNTY

| ZONE | USE | DENSITY |
|---|---|---|
| NONURBAN: | | |
| Suburban Estate | Single Family | 35,000 sq. ft./DU |
| Suburban Residential | Single Family | See text |
| Agricultural | Single Family | 10 acres/DU |
| General | Single and Multi-Family | See Text |
| SINGLE FAMILY RESIDENTIAL-URBAN: | | |
| RS-15,000 | Single Family | 3   DU/Acre approx. |
| RS-9,600 | Single Family | 4.5 DU/Acre approx. |
| RS-7,200 | Single Family | 6   DU/Acre approx. |
| DUPLEX: | | |
| RD-3,600 | Duplex | 12  DU/Acre approx. |
| MULTI-FAMILY: | | |
| RM-2,400 | Multi-Family | 18  DU/Acre approx. |
| RM-1,800 | Multi-Family | 24  DU/Acre approx. |
| RM- 900 | Multi-Family Hotels, Motels, Offices, Trailer Parks | 48  DU/Acre approx. |

uses specified generally cumulate downward, so that the more
protected single family residential uses are allowed in the less
restrictive multi-family classifications. But note that a change in
use generally involves a change in density, with the multi-family
zones carrying the higher densities. In effect, then, we concentrate on rezonings which contemplate an increase in density to
allow apartment development. We will treat as an apartment
rezoning any rezoning in which land not previously in an apartment classification is shifted to a zone which permits multi-
family development. Usually, these shifts require a change from
a nonurban residential or urban residential zone to apartment
development, treating the duplex as single-family development
for our purposes. (There were few shifts from duplex zoning in
our sample.) There are a few complications, however, which
must briefly be mentioned:

1. Two of the nonurban zones present problems. The suburban residential zone requires five acres for each dwelling unit,
but permits conversion to higher densities if public facilities are
available. This zone was considered a transitional zone by the
planning department, but is limited to single family development. A shift from this category to apartment zoning will be
considered a rezoning to apartments for purposes of our study.
The General zone does permit multi-family development at the
lowest multi-family density, but also permits single family uses.
As there were no cases in the study in which the original zoning
was in the General classification, it need not trouble us further.

2. The highest density multi-family zone also permits uses
which are not multi-family. However, discussion with the planning staff indicated that most of the rezonings to this zone were
for multi-family development, and as the zone primarily authorizes multi-family development it has been so treated.

A final word is in order on the impact on the zoning process
of the availability of a complementary method of carrying out
land development, known as the planned unit development
method. The essence of the planned unit development technique is that it permits modification of the customary bulk,
siting, and density requirements of the zoning ordinance, provided the development is approved and carried out on the basis
of a plan for development which covers the entire project area.
Allowable densities within the planned unit development may

be increased, or they may simply be shifted within the project, with dwelling units more crowded on the land in return for the provision of common open space elsewhere in the project to compensate for higher densities at selected points. What happens is that the planning agency is willing to trade off greater freedom and less onerous restrictions for the developer in return for the greater opportunities for departmental supervision and imaginative planning which the planned unit development presents. Especially in rapidly urbanizing areas such as King County, the planned unit development process is seen as a method of achieving higher standards of site design and a protection of site amenities, all of which enhance the attractiveness of the project.

King County had added a planned development procedure to its zoning ordinance at the time of this study, and probably led the northwest in its use. It must be stressed, however, that the planned development technique does not necessarily require a rezone change. Many planned developments included only single family dwellings, and were carried out in areas already zoned for single family uses. Since apartment development generally required a rezone, however, any planned development including apartments had to be preceded by a rezone amendment. In these cases, the planning department had decided that the zone change should be applied for and granted before the developer proceeded to the design of his project. This procedure roughly parallels the two-step process which the author has recommended elsewhere,[183] separating as it does the decision on the qualitative changes which need legislative approval from the design of the project, which can properly be left to the planning commission. No attempt was made to study planned unit developments for apartments in detail, but on the assumption that the planners and perhaps the commission and board would be more sympathetic to a rezone which was followed by a planned unit development, these cases were isolated for separate study.

## The Apartment Rezoning Study

We are now ready to look more closely at our apartment zoning study, and what it shows about the implementation of

---

[183] D. Mandelker, Controlling Planned Residential Developments (1966).

planning and zoning policy in the King County setting. The aim of the study was to analyze and appraise apartment rezonings in the county on the basis of the criteria used by the zoning agencies, much as a lawyer would review and appraise the decisions of an appellate court over a given period of time. For this study, 170 apartment rezoning applications were selected, covering those cases which first appeared on the monthly agenda of the planning commission in the one year period from September, 1967, through September, 1968, although in some cases final action on the rezone took place after the cutoff date. As these rezone applications were considered during the recent period of increased apartment construction, the number and volume of the cases is sufficiently large to give us a good representation of King County zoning policies as they were carried out in action.

We have already noted that the comprehensive plan selected a series of criteria which were to be considered by the zoning agencies when making decisions on proposed apartment rezones. Our purpose in this study is to determine, if possible, which of these criteria did in fact have a substantial influence on the zoning outcome in the cases in our sample. To carry out this inquiry, a user-oriented computer analysis system was employed which was in the process of development at the Urban Data Center of the University of Washington. Known as System X, the system was adaptable to the operations required by the study since it was able to produce two-way, cross-tabular comparisons of selected variables which were thought to have an influence on the zoning result. The system also produced computer-drawn plots of approved and disapproved rezones which permitted the results of the rezoning process to be matched with the urban center locations selected by the comprehensive plan.

We must next explain some of the assumptions of our study which qualify our interpretation of the data but which, we submit, are not sufficiently heroic to seriously detract from our results! The 170 cases in the sample aggregated 1,239 acres or approximately two square miles in area, and with apartment densities averaging twenty dwelling units to the acre, the area proposed for rezoning had a potential holding capacity in the neighborhood of 24,780 units. Considering the short period of time involved, the potential net addition to King County population was substantial—at least 75,000, assuming an average of three persons per dwelling unit. It would have been possible, though difficult, to trace the subsequent history of rezones granted in our sample to find those cases in which apartment development actually followed the rezone approval. But we were not primarily interested in the subsequent history of our study cases, as our concern was with the substantive basis on which zoning decisions were being made. Nonetheless, one of the striking findings of the study was the presence in the county of large numbers of apartment (and business) rezones in which no development had occurred at the time a subsequent apartment rezone in the same area was presented for consideration. We should not be surprised by this discovery, for we had suggested that the stockpiling of rezoned tracts would characterize any developmental setting in which zoning changes were essential to the land development process. Nonetheless, the criteria in the plan had not taken account of this possibility, a state of affairs (as we have suggested) which seriously affects the ability of the zoning agencies to control development priorities. Much of our concern will be with the influence of undeveloped rezones on zoning decisions, and with the reaction of the zoning agencies to this problem.

We must next make explicit a decision that was made in utilizing the information in the zoning files. These files contained a map of the rezone site and the surrounding area, a full report on the rezone proposal by the planning department, and the findings of the commission and of the board, when an appeal to the board was taken. For the most part, the findings of the commission and the board were brief and in standardized form, a practice common in local zoning procedure. For this reason, we did not rely primarily on the verbalized reasons given by the zoning agencies when examining the basis for their decisions. Instead, information about the rezone site and the area around it was used as the basis for determining whether the record of the zoning agencies was faithful to the zoning criteria of the comprehensive plan. In other words, we have made the assumption that since the zoning criteria in the plan were expressed in terms of physical, environmental characteristics, the zoning record can be judged in these environmental terms. Fortunately, as we will see, the reasons for the zoning result were expressed more carefully in many of the cases in which there appears to have been a departure from the comprehensive plan's guidelines. In these cases, we will also make use of the reasons given for the zoning action.

In making our evaluation, we rely heavily on the information in the formal zoning record. We are relatively confident in doing so because, as we have seen, the amendment process was utilized to secure zoning changes to allow apartments, and practically all of these changes were initiated by developers. What the study cannot pick up, of course, are the applicants who were discouraged by planning department staff from entering the rezone process in the first instance. But it was the informal policy of the planning department to encourage developers to make application, partly because the planners saw the rezone process as a necessary test of the policies contained in the comprehensive plan. Subject to this qualification, what strikes the observer about the rezone process is its comparative visibility. There is little evidence of collaboration between the planning department and planning commission to shunt the developer around the zoning system to frustrate his ambitions. Nor is there much evidence of developer applications at very high densities with the anticipation that the zoning agencies could be bargained down to lower, but still acceptable, levels. Bargaining of this sort had occurred at one time, but by the time of this study another policy—again informal—had been adopted that called for denial of an application from a developer who attempted to bargain with the zoning agencies. In the study sample there were a few cases in which requested zoning densities were reduced in the approval process, but they are rare. Another observation is of some interest. Planning department staff were candid in admitting that apartment proposals which met the test of the plan were subject to denial if the planning department was unhappy with the applicant, his past performance, or his willingness to work with it. But the open and public nature of the hearings before the commission and the board prevented the staff from communicating this information upward, so that amendment proposals were decided by the commission and the board on the basis of the information presented at their hearings. New procedures now under development are intended to remove any opportunity for injecting personal considerations into decisions on zoning applications.

We should also comment on what effect the size of the rezone site had on our evaluation. Since the comprehensive plan singled out several characteristics in the area surrounding the rezone site as factors to be considered, our evaluation concentrated on the development and zoning found adjacent to the rezone. As this evaluation was based on the map which was part of the zoning file, the larger the rezone site the larger the area surrounding the site that was included in the map. We feel, however, that the important element was the relationship between the site and the surrounding area, so that the actual size of the site is of secondary importance. Moreover, an inspection of the study sample indicates that while the median size of an apartment rezone site was 2.5 acres, all but twenty-two of the sites were under fifteen acres, a range narrow enough to make the areas included in the 170 zoning maps reasonably comparable.

## *Implementing the Urban Centers Concept*

Let us now turn to our zoning study to see how the zoning record conformed to the urban centers concept which had been proposed by the comprehensive plan. We have already noted that the computer was programmed to plot zoning approvals and disapprovals in the study sample. As relationship to arterials was so important an element, both in the urban centers and apartment rezoning policies, these plots were superimposed on the King County transportation system map. The next three maps show, in turn, the apartment rezones finally approved after the zoning process and all appeals were completed, the apartment rezones initially denied by the planning department, and the apartment rezones approved by the planning commission and the board of county commissioners over the planning department's disapproval.

Before we turn to an interpretation of the maps, however, we must indicate the way in which the rezone sites were plotted. These sites were first located at the center of the government survey sections in which they were found, with a further separation of sites within the same section to avoid overprinting. Site location is thus generalized by survey section, and the locations are approximate. There are other limitations to the maps. As our study covered only one year of rezone activity, the maps do not show the relation of rezones approved in this period to centers of high-intensity development which existed before our study period began. In addition, the effect of not distinguishing between large and small sites must be recognized, since the larger sites will have a greater impact on the implementation of the urban centers policy. At the same time, including the smaller sites corrects somewhat for the restrictiveness of the sample, since some of the smaller rezoning applications in the study period occurred in areas in which apartment development had already taken place.

Even with these limitations, the picture portrayed by the maps is striking. We might begin with Map 6, which shows the results of the zoning process after all appeals had been taken. This map shows surprising fidelity to the urban centers concept, as approved apartment development tends to be grouped in areas which had been earmarked by the plan as urban centers. Development does tend to be more scattered along radial arterials than might have been expected, but close relationship to the arterial system is at least consistent with the plan's reliance on highway proximity as a basis for apartment rezones.

If we look next at the other two maps we find some other significant results. Map 7 shows the rezones denied by the planning department, and we would expect these sites not to be related to proposed urban centers. An inspection of the map does indicate, in general, that apartment rezones denied by the planning department tend to be more scattered than those which were finally approved in the rezone process. But there are also apartment rezone sites at or near suggested centers of urban concentration which the planning department denied. We will come back to these cases later.

Finally, Map 8 shows those planning department denials reversed by the planning commission and the board of county commissioners. If we can generalize at all about the location of these sites, they tend to appear at those very points of concentration which the comprehensive plan had selected. They also tend, though marginally, to be more scattered and peripheral to the central urban core than do all of the sites in the entire study

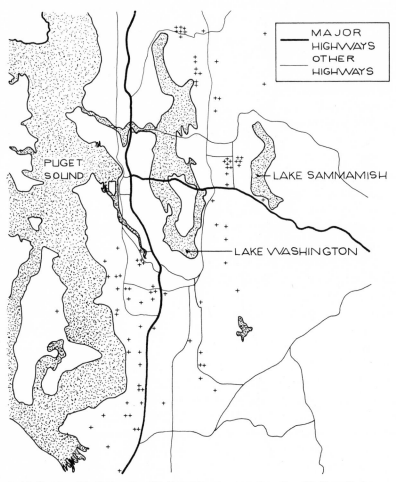

MAP 6: APARTMENT REZONE APPLICATIONS (+)
    FINALLY APPROVED.

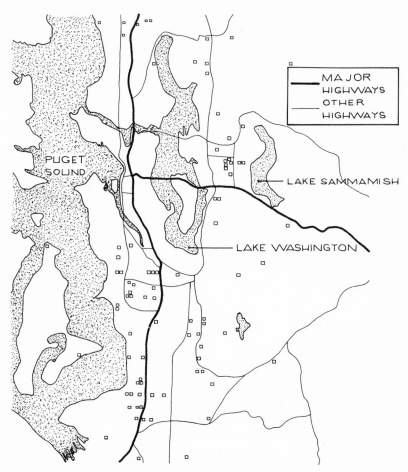

MAP 7: APARTMENT REZONE APPLICATIONS (□) DENIED
BY KING COUNTY PLANNING DEPARTMENT.

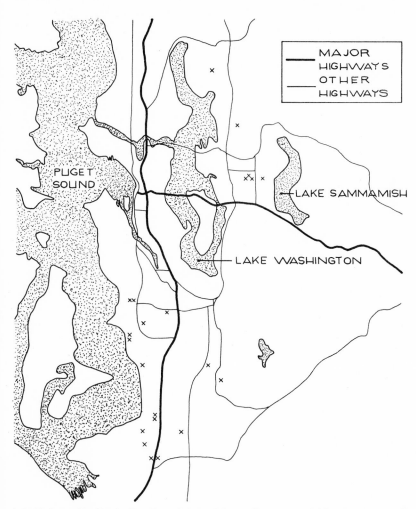

MAP 8: APARTMENT REZONES APPROVED (×)BY PLANNING
COMMISSION AND BOARD OF COUNTY COMMISSIONERS
OVER PLANNING DEPARTMENT DISAPPROVAL.

sample. This finding would suggest that one effect of planning commission and board action on the rezone proposals was to move potential development centers further out into the county, a tendency which is contrary to and not in accordance with the plan's encouragement of more concentrated patterns. This attitude in the board and the commission will also be examined in more detail later in this chapter.

So far, we have been looking at the computer-drawn maps as evidence of the fidelity of the zoning process to the proposals of the comprehensive plan. Let us now turn the analysis around. How useful was the plan in providing guidance to the zoning system? We might begin this discussion by noting that our maps revealed apparent inconsistencies in comparatively circumscribed areas, such as the area between the two lakes, where even the planning department seems inconsistent in what appears to be closely related locations. Closer inspection of the files indicated that zoning conflicts within limited areas were not as common as the maps might suggest, since the scale of the maps is too large to pick up the neighborhood boundaries that are crucial to the zoning decision. Nevertheless, what created difficulties for the computer also created difficulties for the implementation of the comprehensive plan. Apparent inconsistency in the zoning record in the same area may only reflect the limited usefulness of a countywide comprehensive plan for a zoning process which must deal piecemeal with relatively small sites. The plan attempted to deal with this problem by delineating a model for physical development at the neighborhood scale, but it did not provide the necessary policy linkages between the neighborhood model and the community-wide planning framework. For example, the schematic indication of location points for urban centers was simply not detailed enough to indicate the boundaries of those urban centers that were to be preferred in the zoning process. This omission created an ambiguity and tension in the zoning system, which found itself caught between the more specific development criteria for limited neighborhoods, and the broader developmental framework that was projected for the entire county. We will see these ambiguities and tensions reflected in a more detailed examination of the record of the zoning agencies, to which we now turn.

*Relating the Zoning Record to the Plan*

Table 2 compares the approval record on apartment rezones of each of the King County zoning agencies. The results confirm the folklore of zoning, which has it that the lay zoning agencies are more responsive to development pressures from the private market than professional planners. While the planning department would have denied a majority of the applications, this ratio was reversed before the commission and the board, each approving a majority of the rezone proposals. This decision record is more completely analyzed in Tables 3 through 5. We would expect from Table 2 that many planning department denials would have been reversed, but now we note that most of these reversals occurred before the commission, not the board. In 23 cases in which the planning department denied the application the planning commission approved 18 and denied five, but these five cases were appealed to the board, which reversed both the commission and the planners and approved the rezones. Note that board reversal of cases in which both the commission and the planners had denied the rezone runs counter to the informal understanding, that the board would concur in the result when both the commission and the planners were in agreement. These five reversals occurred late in the study period, reinforcing an observation by King County planners that the board had decided at this point to depart from its informal policy of not reversing when both planners and the commission had agreed. We might also note that rezone approvals make up a greater proportion of the appeals to the board than rezone denials, so that we could have expected an even more favorable record before the board if even more denials had been appealed to it.

We cannot accept this record uncritically, however, for a more lenient attitude toward developers may not necessarily mean less fidelity to the criteria of the comprehensive plan. An indication of the fidelity of the zoning record to the urban centers concept is provided in our maps of apartment rezone sites. We can now provide a check on faithfulness to the substantive criteria of the plan by relating the substantive apartment zoning criteria specified in the plan to the record of the zoning agencies. For the cases in our sample, two criteria were listed by the

## TABLE 2.  APPROVAL RECORD OF APARTMENT
## REZONES BY DECISION AGENCY*

| APPROVE | DENY | | APPROVAL RATIO |
|---|---|---|---|
| 77 | 93 | PLANNING DEPARTMENT .. | .83 |
| 86 | 84 | PLANNING COMMISSION ... | 1.03 |
| 22 | 17 | BOARD OF COUNTY COMMISSIONERS** ....... | 1.23 |
| 93 | 77 | FINAL OUTCOME ......... | 1.21 |

\* Duplex rezones and withdrawals by the applicant before the planning commission are counted as denials in this and the following tables.
\*\* Four cases were remanded by the board for rehearing.

## TABLE 3.  PLANNING COMMISSION ACTION ON PLAN-
## NING DEPARTMENT RECOMMENDATIONS

PLANNING
COMMISSION:

| | | | |
|---|---|---|---|
| APPROVE | 86 | 18 | 68 |
| DENY | 84 | 75 | 9 |
| | | 93 | 77 |
| PLANNING DEPARTMENT: | | DENY | APPROVE |

## TABLE 4.  BOARD OF COUNTY COMMISSIONERS ACTION ON APPEALS FROM PLANNING COMMISSION

BOARD:

| | | | |
|---|---|---|---|
| REMAND | 4 | 2 | 2 |
| APPROVE | 22 | 7 | 15 |
| DENY | 17 | 17 | 0 |
| | | 26 | 17 |
| PLANNING COMMISSION | | DENY | APPROVE |

## TABLE 5.  BOARD OF COUNTY COMMISSIONERS ACTION ON PLANNING DEPARTMENT RECOMMENDATIONS

BOARD:

| | | | |
|---|---|---|---|
| REMAND | 4 | 2 | 2 |
| APPROVE | 22 | 6 | 16 |
| DENY | 17 | 15 | 2 |
| | | 23 | 20 |
| PLANNING DEPARTMENT | | DENY | APPROVE |

plan as critical to an apartment rezoning—proximity to arterials and a relationship to business centers. We will look closely at the influence of these factors on apartment rezones, but before we do we might look at another factor in our zoning cases which was not explicitly considered by the plan, but which could be expected to have an important effect on the plan's implementation. While no mention was made in the plan of the importance of size of site to the implementation of the urban centers concept, we might suggest nevertheless that, all other factors being equal, the larger sites should have been preferred. Since the plan aimed for high density concentrations, it would seem that committing a larger share of the environment to any one developer at any one strategic location would carry with it a better guarantee that the desired concentration would actually be carried out. We had also suggested that potentially harmful externalities could be handled more easily on the larger site, which should also have been preferred on this basis. Judicial disfavor of "spot" rezonings points in the same direction.

With all of these factors in mind, we find to our surprise that smaller sites fared better than larger sites in the King County zoning process. This information is presented in Tables 6 and 7. Not only did the smaller sites do better, but it would appear that the commission and the board were slightly more responsive to zoning applications on large sites than was the planning department, although this finding must be qualified by the fact that rezones appealed to the board were on the average much larger than the sites on which no appeal was taken—8.8 acres against 6.8 acres. This finding suggests that it may have been the bigger developers with the larger sites who fought their way up to the board of county commissioners. Perhaps the overriding consideration, however, is that the apartment rezones in this study were, as a group, very small. This characteristic presents difficulties for the implementation of a plan which bases its strategies on planning proposals which apply to relatively large areas of land. Our triad of cases which came to the Maryland appellate court from the same highway intersection also dealt with relatively small parcels. If the King County experience is representative, it is not often that a zoning agency can deal at one time with an area which is as significant to the planning concept as the area which was considered in the *Bigenho* case.

## TABLE 6.  DISTRIBUTION OF APARTMENT REZONES BY SIZE OF SITE*

| SIZE IN ACRES | FINALLY APPROVED | FINALLY DENIED |
|---|---|---|
| 2.5 or less | 55 | 30 |
| 15.0 or more | 9 | 13 |

* Sites between 2.5 and 15.0 acres not included.

## TABLE 7.  APARTMENT APPROVAL RECORD BY AVERAGE SIZE OF PARCEL

| | APPROVED | DENIED |
|---|---|---|
| PLANNING DEPARTMENT ACTION | 5.7 acres | 8.6 acres |
| FINAL ACTION FOLLOWING COMMISSION HEARING AND BOARD APPEAL, IF ANY | 6.5 acres | 8.3 acres |

The problem deserves more consideration than it has received.

We turn, then, to a zoning process in which the proposals of the King County plan were implemented in a series of rezones on relatively small parcels. What influence did the apartment zoning criteria selected by the plan have on the zoning results? Let us begin with arterial proximity. Great weight was placed by the comprehensive plan on proximity to arterials as a factor favorable to apartment rezoning, and we have noted that the plan would seem to require arterial proximity at least as a necessary condition to the apartment rezoning. But the application of this standard is not spelled out as much as we would have liked. For example, distance from the arterial is not explicitly considered by the plan, although it would seem to be an important factor to be taken into account. We analyzed the effect of distance from the highway on the zoning result, only to find that practically all of the rezones were abutting or very close to the highway. Even so, this factor had very little influence, as the zoning record after all appeals were taken showed that approvals and disapprovals were about evenly divided even when the rezone site was abutting or near the arterial.

While not considering the distance factor, the plan did consider the relative importance of different highway routes to apartment zoning, and did attempt some classification along these lines. For example, we noted that Interstate highways and expressways were not listed as arterials along which apartment development was favored, and that the planners made this omission because these highways do not afford direct access. Remember also that the plan distinguished major and secondary routes, with an emphasis on higher density development adjacent to the major arterials. This distinction does not appear as a factor in the consideration of the zoning applications, however, and we have not pursued it. Probably the failure of developers fully to utilize the higher densities made these differentiations less important than they appeared when the plan was prepared.

However incomplete the policies of the comprehensive plan on the importance of arterial proximity to apartment rezoning, Table 8 would indicate that this factor had a limited influence on the zoning outcome. Whatever the classification of the high- way which was nearest the rezoning site, the number of approvals and disapprovals was about evenly balanced. Note, however,

## TABLE 8.  INFLUENCE OF ARTERIAL CHARACTER ON APARTMENT REZONES

| ARTERIAL | FINAL OUTCOME | | PLANNING DEPARTMENT | | PLANNING COMMISSION | | BOARD OF COMMISSIONERS | |
|---|---|---|---|---|---|---|---|---|
| | APPROVE | DENY | APPROVE | DENY | APPROVE | DENY | APPROVE | DENY |
| INTERSTATE | 10 | 9 | 9 | 10 | 10 | 9 | 2 | 3 |
| MAJOR | 52 | 34 | 37 | 49 | 49 | 37 | 13 | 5 |
| SECONDARY | 23 | 23 | 23 | 23 | 21 | 25 | 5 | 7 |
| NONE | 8 | 11 | 8 | 11 | 6 | 13 | 2 | 4 |

a considerable shift toward a more favorable result before the planning commission in those cases in which the nearest highway was a major arterial. *This is the greatest interagency shift in rezone result in the entire study.* On its face, this finding would suggest that the planning commission was to this extent more faithful to the plan than the planners, since proximity to a major arterial was listed as an important factor favorable to a rezoning. But this difference in attitude was explained by the planners, who indicated that they qualified the criteria of the plan by demanding more than arterial proximity to justify a rezone. Some relationship to business centers was also required, consistent with the plan's emphasis on complementary development.

We can test the explanation offered by the planners by looking at those twelve cases in which an initial denial by the planning department of an apartment rezone near a major highway was reversed by the planning commission. Here we find that the character of the surrounding development was as follows:

Single family or undeveloped . . 6
Business . . . . . . . . . . . . . . 4
Apartment . . . . . . . . . . . . . 2

In those cases in which there was adjacent business development it would seem that the planners should have granted the rezoning. Where the surroundings were undeveloped or single family, the initial judgment by the planners would appear correct. But we discover another surprising result when we look at the character of the zoning which was adjacent to the sites in these cases:

Apartment . . . . . . . . . . . . . 9
Business . . . . . . . . . . . . . . 1
Low density residential . . . . . . 2

Since proximity to a major arterial appears to be a necessary but not a sufficient condition to an apartment rezone, those cases in which there was a shift in zoning result before the planning commission provide a clue to the area of disagreement between the commission and the planning department. Since most of the planning department reversals occurred before the commission, it is the difference in attitude between these two agencies which demands the closest exploration. These twelve cases adjacent to major arterials in which the planning department was reversed suggest that this action by the commission was accompanied by a more favorable attitude toward apartment rezones in the comparatively undeveloped areas of the county, contrary to the intention of the plan. In the pages that follow, we intend to investigate these differences in attitude more closely, paying special attention to the influence of surrounding uses on the apartment rezone proposals.

But notice that we have introduced another factor for consideration—the effect that adjacent zoning had on the apartment zoning application. An examination of the twelve major arterial cases in which a shift occurred indicates that, in many of the cases in which the surrounding uses were comparatively undeveloped, there were adjacent apartment zones which had been approved but which had not been utilized. This possibility—the banking of rezones against future needs—was predicted by our model of the zoning process, but was not foreseen in the preparation of the King County comprehensive plan. It is a feature of the land development process which bears examination, and for this reason we have extended the criteria of the plan by adding an analysis of adjacent zoning as it affected the zoning record.

Tables 9 and 10 summarize the influence of adjacent use and adjacent zoning on the zoning results. They appear on page 148 and page 151. We will next analyze their meaning in some detail, but it is first fair to ask whether the distribution of approvals and disapprovals in these tables has statistical significance on which we can rely in making our evaluation. To make this determination a conventional Chi Square analysis was applied to each table. We wanted to know, for each of the zoning agencies, and for the final outcome of the zoning process once all appeals had been taken, whether the three classifications of adjacent use and the three classifications of adjacent zoning had a significant influence on the zoning result. In other words, did it make a difference for the zoning result whether the area surrounding the rezone site fell in one of these three categories?

The results of the Chi Square analysis are presented in Appendix B to this chapter.* It indicates that the different categories of adjacent use and adjacent zoning were significant to the decision record of the planning department and the planning commission, but not to the decision record of the board of county commissioners. Some reasons are advanced in Appendix B why the findings for the board were inconclusive. Here the point to make is that the Chi Square findings do indicate a comparatively high degree of fidelity at least to the surrounding use component of the comprehensive plan criteria. For example, most apartment rezonings in single family or undeveloped areas were denied. Most apartment rezonings adjacent to business development were approved. Once more, however, shifts toward a more favorable attitude appear in undeveloped areas, and in cases in which unused apartment zoning was near the site of the zoning application which was under consideration. To understand why these changes occurred, and what they illustrate about the zoning process, we turn next to a more detailed analysis of the influence of adjacent use and adjacent zoning on the decision record.

## Adjacent Uses and Adjacent Zoning

Let us look first at the influence of adjacent use on the zoning result. While the adjacent uses coded for computer analysis were more finely differentiated initially, the distribution of the rezones in the sample, and similarities in the categories, permitted three general use combinations which were employed in our analysis. The categories follow:

*Single Family or Undeveloped.* In these cases, either the area surrounding the rezone site was undeveloped, the site was surrounded by single family uses, or there was a combination of single family residential development and undeveloped territory.

*Apartment.* In this category the surrounding area, whatever its character, contained some apartment development.

---

* *Infra* p. 179.

*Business.* In this category, the area surrounding the rezone site contained some business development. If the area contained apartment development as well it was still placed in this category. A few cases in which the adjacent use was not in one of these categories have been excluded.

An analysis of adjacent use in relation to the zoning record is contained in Table 9. Looking first at the planning department record, we find that the planners favored rezones adjacent to business uses and disfavored rezones when the adjacent use was in the single family or undeveloped category, a record that is reasonably faithful to the guidelines of the plan even though the approval and disapproval ratios are not as significant as we would have expected. Note, again, the more favorable attitude of both the commission and board when the surrounding area was single family or undeveloped. Note also the significantly larger size of the rezone sites in single family and undeveloped areas, which is not unexpected, and the slightly larger proportion of applications in this group which were appealed to the board, a tendency which suggests pressures by developers against the more concentrated developmental policies of the plan.

*Adjacent Zoning.* Let us now turn to adjacent zoning, and we might now state in greater detail the nature of our interest in the influence of adjacent zoning on the zoning record, even though adjacent zoning was not treated as one of the determinative factors by the comprehensive plan. One point is that the character of the area surrounding the rezone site arguably is influenced as much by the zoning as it is by the actual use. Indeed, decisions under the zoning ordinance, as they shake off the limitation of nuisance law to a consideration of existing development, should arguably take their cue from the character of the surrounding zoning more than from the character of the surrounding use. We also noted earlier that the number of outstanding but undeveloped rezonings in relationship to the demand for new development was an important control on the zoning process, and an indicator to which the zoning agencies should be sensitive. Moreover, we noted that holding rezoned areas for future development can weaken the implementation of the plan, since it hinders the fulfillment of the zoning decision, once it has been made. What should the zoning agencies do in

## TABLE 9. INFLUENCE OF ADJACENT USE ON APARTMENT REZONES

| AVERAGE SIZE OF SITE (ACRES) | ADJACENT USE | FINAL OUTCOME | | PLANNING DEPARTMENT | | PLANNING COMMISSION | | BOARD OF COMMISSIONERS | |
|---|---|---|---|---|---|---|---|---|---|
| | | APPROVE | DENY | APPROVE | DENY | APPROVE | DENY | APPROVE | DENY |
| 9.4 | SINGLE FAMILY OR UNDEVELOPED | 43 | 54 | 30 | 67 | 38 | 59 | 12 | 11 |
| 6.2 | APARTMENT | 8 | 8 | 7 | 9 | 8 | 8 | 1 | 1 |
| 3.0 | BUSINESS | 41 | 15 | 40 | 16 | 39 | 17 | 9 | 5 |

these circumstances? For example, in the King County setting, what if there is a rezoning for business which has not yet been developed? Arguably, the presence of business zoning can justify a related apartment development, but the purpose of the plan will be frustrated if the business that is zoned is never built, or is delayed.

We were quite interested, therefore, in the influence of adjacent zoning on the apartment zoning process in King County. We might first indicate how the nature of the adjacent zoning was determined. In each of the cases in the study sample, the apartment rezone site was carved from an existing zone which, with few exceptions, was a low density, single family zone. In ten per cent or so of the cases there was no other zoning adjacent to the rezone site; in these cases the zoning presently in force on the site was also adjacent to it. In all of the other cases, there was zoning adjacent to the rezone site which was different from the zoning on the site itself. In these cases, adjacent zoning was defined as the most important zoning classification surrounding and contiguous to the rezone site. The adjacent classifications coded into the data each represented one of the zones in the zoning ordinance, but they were again combined for purposes of analysis into three categories—low density residential, business, and apartment. A few cases in which the adjacent zoning was not in one of these categories have been excluded.

Some difficulties arose in making the adjacent zoning determination which must now be noted. Often there was a heavy mixture of zones in the vicinity of the rezone site, and in these cases the zone selected as the adjacent zone was the zoning classification closest to the rezone site and which appeared most dominant. But this evaluation was highly subjective, and especially difficult to make when both apartment and business rezones appeared on the map. To correct for the subjective nature of this evaluation, the business and apartment adjacent zoning cases are later combined for analysis as a group.

Thirty-two cases in which the rezone site was contiguous to another municipality were more troublesome. The planning department report covered uses in a contiguous municipality, but not the zoning classifications. Adjacent zoning designations do not, for this reason, reflect the zoning in the contiguous municipality, a limitation qualified by the fact that the rezone site usually bordered the contiguous municipality on one side only, and by the circumstance that the rezone decision was based on the county zoning plan and ordinance even though the contiguous community was consulted.

Table 10 shows the influence of adjacent zoning on the apartment zoning results. Since the effect of adjacent zoning was not explicitly considered by the comprehensive plan, the table is not that easy to evaluate. However, the generally unfavorable action on apartment rezones when the surrounding area was zoned low density residential, as compared with the generally favorable reaction on apartment rezones when the surrounding area was zoned business, tends to square with the plan's emphasis on the urban centers concept. What is most striking about the table is the reaction of the different zoning agencies in those cases in which the surrounding zoning was for apartment uses. In these cases the balance of approvals to disapprovals was reversed as the applications went through the zoning process, with most of the reversals occurring before the planning commission. We might get a better perspective on what this shift in attitude meant to the zoning record by comparing the distribution of zoning sites in Table 10 with the distribution of zoning sites in Table 9. What immediately strikes us is that most of the rezones in the sample tended to be located in areas in which the *uses* were undeveloped or low density, but in which the adjacent *zoning* was business or multi-family. We might pursue our analysis of the zoning record by looking more closely at this relationship.

## The Zoning Record in Undeveloped Areas

Table 11 compares adjacent uses with adjacent zoning in more detail. In 51 of the 96 cases in which the area adjacent to the rezone site was undeveloped, the adjacent zoning was either business or apartment. The actions of the zoning agencies in these 51 cases are presented in Table 12. In 16 cases in which the surrounding uses fell in the single family or undeveloped category, an initial denial by the planning department was reversed by the commission or board. There was adjacent but

## TABLE 10. INFLUENCE OF ADJACENT ZONING ON APARTMENT REZONES

| AVERAGE SIZE OF SITE (ACRES) | ADJACENT ZONING | FINAL OUTCOME | | PLANNING DEPARTMENT | | PLANNING COMMISSION | | BOARD OF COMMISSIONERS | |
|---|---|---|---|---|---|---|---|---|---|
| | | APPROVE | DENY | APPROVE | DENY | APPROVE | DENY | APPROVE | DENY |
| 10.6 | LOW DENSITY RESIDENTIAL | 17 | 36 | 14 | 39 | 15 | 38 | 7 | 8 |
| 7.2 | BUSINESS | 32 | 13 | 28 | 17 | 29 | 16 | 6 | 5 |
| 4.6 | APARTMENT | 43 | 26 | 33 | 36 | 40 | 29 | 8 | 4 |

## TABLE 11. RELATIONSHIP BETWEEN ADJACENT USE AND ADJACENT ZONING*

ADJACENT ZONING:**

| | SINGLE FAMILY | UNDEVELOPED | APARTMENT | BUSINESS |
|---|---|---|---|---|
| APARTMENT | 69 | 36 | 13 | 20 |
| BUSINESS | 45 | 15 | 0 | 30 |
| LOW DENSITY RESIDENTIAL | 53 | 45 | 3 | 5 |
| | | 96 | 16 | 55 |

ADJACENT USE:

* Totals exclude three cases in which the adjacent zoning was manufacturing.

** Recall that this is the most significant adjacent zoning classification.

TABLE 12. ACTION OF ZONING AGENCIES WHEN
APARTMENT OR BUSINESS ZONING IS
ADJACENT BUT ADJACENT USE IS
RESIDENTIAL OR UNDEVELOPED

|  | APPROVE | DISAPPROVE |
|---|---|---|
| PLANNING DEPARTMENT | 19 | 32 |
| PLANNING COMMISSION | 26 | 25 |
| BOARD OF COMMISSIONERS* | 5 | 4 |

* There was one remand.

undeveloped business or apartment zoning in all but three of
these cases. In other words, the commission and the board were
more willing to extend the external economies which prior zoning for a more intensive use had injected into the environment.
We should not be surprised that the lay agencies would be more
responsive than the planners to private pressures to capitalize on
these development opportunities.

We should next point out that the mere fact that an area is
presently undeveloped or is presently zoned for low intensity
uses is not necessarily conclusive against apartment zoning and
the development of one of the plan's urban centers at that
point. Urban centers might have been designated at strategic
arterial points in undeveloped areas. Unfortunately, the plan as
we have seen was less than attentive to this possibility, though it
did recommend that its urban centers be built on existing developments. This comment would appear to rule out urban centers, and their attendant apartment zones, in undeveloped areas.

With this comment in mind, let us look at those cases in
which the surrounding area was single family or undeveloped, in
which there was no adjacent business or apartment zoning, but
in which a planning department denial was reversed by the commission or the board. Only three cases are in this group. Arguably, in view of what we have said, these cases are improper

spot zonings not in accordance with the criteria of the plan. Their characteristics are given in Figure 3. To some extent, facts not picked up by the coding system explain the results, and indicate that some attention was in fact paid to the planning criteria. In the first two cases, the agency approving the rezone emphasized the topographical separation of the rezone site from the surrounding area, thus applying a compatibility test at the neighborhood scale to find no harmful externality. Moreover, the rezone site in the first case was comparatively large, and the board relied on this fact when granting the rezone. As we have suggested, a large enough rezone can create its own urban center. In the second case, the apartment rezone was near a business center in another municipality, and this point was stressed even though the distance from the business area would seem to foreclose approval under the urban centers concept. Finally, the third case included a request for business development jointly with the apartment rezone. As we point out below, joint business development concurrent with an apartment rezone request can be considered faithful to the urban centers concept. The trouble is that the plan, by stressing existing proximate business development, is not sensitive to the possibilities for plan implementation through joint business-residential proposals.

So far we have been looking at cases in single family or undeveloped areas in which an initial denial by the planning department was reversed by the commission and the board, and we have been trying to determine what zoning or planning attitudes might have influenced these reversals. We might get another perspective on this problem by looking at those cases in which the surrounding use was single family or undeveloped but in which there was *no* adjacent business or apartment zoning. We would expect that *all* of these cases would be *denied* by *all* of the zoning agencies. There were 35 cases in this group, and while all of the zoning agencies agreed in denying the rezone in 24 of these cases, in 11 of these cases the planning department itself granted the rezone, and was reversed in only one instance.

Let us look at these cases more closely. In the 24 denials, the department and the commission agreed on all 24; five were appealed all the way to the board, and the board upheld the denial in all five. A close inspection of these cases indicates that practically all of them were clearly isolated rezoning proposals

## FIGURE 3. APPROVALS BY COMMISSION AND BOARD IN SINGLE FAMILY AND UNDEVELOPED AREAS IN ABSENCE OF ADJACENT BUSINESS OR APARTMENT ZONING

| CASE | ZONING ON SITE | SIZE OF SITE | PLANNING DEPT. | PLANNING COMMN. | BOARD OF COMM'RS | ARTERIAL |
|------|----------------|--------------|----------------|-----------------|------------------|----------|
| No. 1 | SR* | 15.0 | Deny | Deny | Approve | None |
| No. 2 | High-Density* single family | 2.0 | Deny | Approve | No appeal | Major |
| No. 3 | High-Density single family** | 4.3 | Deny | Approve | No appeal | Major |

*  No other adjacent zoning.

** In this case the adjacent zoning was the lowest-density single family classification.

in rural areas, unrelated to existing or potential business centers, or even to zoned or developed apartment areas. Indeed, one-third of these cases arose under the old zoning code, which as we have indicated covered the outer or unurbanized reaches of the county. This fact alone is significant. In one of these cases there was undeveloped business zoning in the vicinity. It was not picked up in the computer coding, and an inspection of the map indicates that single family zoning was dominant, an inference supported by the decision of the zoning agencies to credit the single family classification as the major zoning influence.

As far as we have come, we have at least noted planning department consistency to the principles of the plan to the extent that the department was usually unwilling to grant apartment rezones in undeveloped or lightly developed areas of the county. What about the eleven cases in which the adjacent use was single family or undeveloped, in which there was no adjacent apartment or business zoning, and in which the planning department *granted* the apartment rezone? While these cases were superficially decided contrary to the plan, a closer inspection of the files indicates redeeming features which give consistency to the planning department record. We have noted in these cases that no adjacent business or apartment zoning was coded for computer analysis. In some apartment zoning applications, however, the applicant would sometimes ask jointly for an apartment or business rezone, or would apply for apartment zoning in the context of a planned unit development, which permitted a more comprehensive review of the zoning application by the planning department. In the total study sample there are 23 such planned unit or joint development cases, and five are found in this group of 11 in which the planning department approved the rezone in what appeared to be an undeveloped or single family area. Strictly speaking, a joint application for apartment and business zoning cannot be coded as an adjacent business zoning because the business zoning was not in existence at the time the apartment rezone application was made. Nevertheless, approval of the apartment rezone in connection with a business rezone would appear consistent with the policies of the comprehensive plan. On the other hand, approval of an apartment rezone as part of a planned unit development simply underscores the more favorable attitude of the planners toward rezones which are part of the planned unit development process. Other characteristics of these 11 cases are also interesting. In two of them the rezone site had potentially been rezoned for apartment uses. A potential zoning designation is an innovation in the King County zoning ordinance, which treats the potential zone designation as presumptively indicating a justification for a zone change.[184] The study sample itself contained thirty cases in which there was a potential zone, and in these the applicant was more than 90 per cent successful.

Apart from joint applications for business development, application for a planned unit development concurrent with the apartment rezone request, and zoning designations presumptively indicating a rezone change, there were a few cases in which the planning department relied on development patterns throughout the general area surrounding the rezone site, and which could not have been picked up by the coding system used for the computer analysis. In these cases the department found either that the area had generally been committed to apartment development, or that the area was adjacent to a nearby business center. What is significant is that the planning department, in approving rezones in what looked like undeveloped areas, fell back on the guidelines of the comprehensive plan and considered an area wider than the vicinity of the rezone site to justify its decision. We have noticed something of the same tendency in court decisions that consider the validity of apartment rezonings that are challenged by neighbors. It is also significant that, in one of the cases in which the planning department took this attitude, the planning commission reversed the department on the ground that the rezone was not adequately buffered from the surrounding single family development. Apart from this one case, all of the other rezones in this group were affirmed on appeal, five of them going to the board of commissioners, a much higher proportion of appeals than in the total sample.

### The Zoning Record as Influenced by Adjacent Business or Apartment Uses

So far we have been examining rezoning applications in which the area surrounding the rezone site would indicate that

---

[184] Zoning Code § 24.46.060.

the rezone should be denied. We look next at a group of cases which did not arise in single family or undeveloped areas, but in areas in which business uses were adjacent to the proposed apartment rezone. Even though the plan would indicate that the rezoning in these cases should have been granted, not only did the planning department deny 16 of these applications, but only a few of these denials were reversed either by the commission or the board. Since the record of all of the zoning agencies was remarkably consistent in these cases, we might look at the planning department justifications for the zoning denials as representative of the zoning attitude.

Here an inspection of the files produces a set of zoning justifications which are difficult to classify. The overriding impression is that the planning department relied on considerations which were related to the immediate area surrounding the rezone site, at a level too localized to have been picked up by the comprehensive plan. For example, there are cases in which a comprehensive zoning study was under way, or in which the history of zoning in the area, carrying implications of an administrative *res judicata*, led to the denial. In other cases, topographical separations between the apartment rezoning and the business development were put forward to justify the denial, and in others the business development was found to be too far away. Reliance on distance as a reason for denying the rezone is hard to line up with reliance on distant business centers to justify the rezone in other cases in which the immediate area was undeveloped. What appears from the files is an implicit selection of a limited number of business areas for additional development for apartment use, a basis for decision arguably consistent with the plan's selection of only a limited number of urban concentration points, but one which was not made explicit in the plan itself.

Finally, what about those cases in which there was an apartment use adjacent to the rezone site, but in which the planning department refused the rezone? The nine cases in this group have interesting characteristics. In practically all of them the adjacent zoning was also for apartments, and in some of these cases the planning department did give as its reason a desire to limit the extension of apartment development. In other cases the department found lack of access to an arterial or lack of proximity to business as a reason for denial, and it is also interesting to note that in none of these cases was business development proposed jointly with the apartment rezone. In three of the cases, however, the planning department's denial was reversed after a hearing by the planning commission.

## Some Final Comments on the Zoning Record

We have concentrated so far on the characteristics of the apartment rezone cases as they have been related to the approval and denial record, with only secondary attention to the influence of different zoning agency reactions on the final outcome. We might now take a closer look at the influence which the commission and board had on the final outcome, by concentrating on those cases in which either the commission or the board reversed a planning department recommendation that came to it. Before doing so, however, we must add one more variable to the decision- making process which might be expected to have an influence on the result, and that variable is public resistance to the rezone change. Claims are quite common in the literature, if not in the myth, of zoning administration that zoning agencies are heavily influenced by public reactions. The claim is advanced, whatever the zoning merits of the proposed change, that the zoning agencies will react negatively whenever sufficient public opposition appears. In this study it was possible to test this hypothesis. The zoning files indicated whether there had been public opposition to the rezone change at the planning commission hearing, or whether neighbors had appealed an apartment rezoning to the board of county commissioners, even though they had not appeared at the commission's public hearing. All of these cases were coded as indicating public opposition to the rezone, and analysis permitted a comparison of the records before the board and commission as they were influenced by public opposition to the zone change. These findings are presented in Table 13. They confirm the zoning myth to the extent that the commission's reaction to rezonings in which there was public opposition was overwhelmingly negative, in spite of the generally favorable position of the commission on the rezonings as a group. To our surprise, however, the board's

## TABLE 13. INFLUENCE OF PUBLIC OPPOSITION TO REZONE CHANGE ON APARTMENT REZONING

| AGENCY | PUBLIC OPPOSITION TO CHANGE | | | |
|---|---|---|---|---|
| | YES | | NO | |
| | APPROVE | DENY | APPROVE | DENY |
| PLANNING COMMISSION | 17 | 42 | 69 | 40 |
| BOARD OF COUNTY COMMISSIONERS | 15 | 11 | 7 | 6 |

record is the other way, and it appears not to have been heavily affected by the public opposition factor.

With this record as a benchmark, we can now look more carefully at the record of the commission and board when they reversed the planning department, testing for the influence of public opposition as well as adjacent use and adjacent zoning on the result. Figures 4, 5, and 6 indicate the characteristics of the rezone cases in three situations in which reversals occurred:

Figure 4. Planning commission denials of planning department approvals.

Figure 5. Planning commission approvals of planning department denials.

Figure 6. Board of commissioners approvals of planning commission denials.

## FIGURE 4. PLANNING COMMISSION DENIALS OF PLANNING DEPARTMENT APPROVALS

| | |
|---|---|
| NUMBER OF CASES | XXXXXXXXX |
| ADJACENT ZONING LOW DENSITY RESIDENTIAL | XXX |
| ADJACENT USE SINGLE FAMILY OR UNDEVELOPED | XXX |
| NO ARTERIAL | XXX |
| PUBLIC OPPOSITION | XXXXXXX |

## FIGURE 5. PLANNING COMMISSION REVERSAL OF PLANNING DEPARTMENT DENIALS

NUMBER OF CASES                  XXXXXXXXXXXXXXXXXX

ADJACENT ZONING
LOW DENSITY
RESIDENTIAL                      XXXX

ADJACENT USE SINGLE
FAMILY OR
UNDEVELOPED                      XXXXXXXXXXX

NO ARTERIAL                      X

PUBLIC OPPOSITION                XXXXXX


## FIGURE 6. BOARD OF COUNTY COMMISSIONERS APPROVAL OF PLANNING COMMISSION DENIALS

NUMBER OF CASES                  XXXXXXX

ADJACENT ZONING LOW
DENSITY RESIDENTIAL              XXX

ADJACENT USE SINGLE
FAMILY OR UNDEVELOPED            XXXXXX

NO ARTERIAL                      XX

PUBLIC OPPOSITION                XXXXX

An examination of these figures reinforces the observations already made. What is striking about the cases in which the planning commission reversed a planning department approval is the large number of cases in which there was public opposition to the rezone, in a group of cases in which the neighborhood around the rezone site was not usually in an undeveloped or single family state. It is of some interest that in two of these cases the board of commissioners reversed the commission on appeal. Three of the other cases in this group were also appealed, a high proportion of appeals which is justified, it would seem, by the character of the area surrounding the rezone site. One of these cases was affirmed by the board, another was remanded, and the third was zoned to duplex use. In cases in which the commission reversed the department, or the board reversed the commission, the outstanding facts are the comparative absence of public opposition in the commission reversals, the high proportion of public opposition in the board reversals, and the general tendency of this group of cases to occur in undeveloped areas or areas in which the surrounding use was residential or undeveloped, a tendency noted in our earlier discussion.

## In Conclusion: Some Lessons of the King County Study

We will not tire the reader with further elaboration of the study data, although Appendix A of this chapter* analyzes the influence on apartment rezoning of the site density change proposed by the zoning applicant. We turn, instead, to some of the tentative conclusions which might be derived from a study limited to a single county, but which nonetheless has produced some significant results. What impresses us immediately are the ambiguities and omissions in the King County comprehensive plan, and in the zoning policies that were adopted to implement the comprehensive plan. The plan compromised. It committed the county to an allocation of urban centers of concentration at specified points at the county level, but at the same time opted for a development model capable of being applied on a neighborhood scale at any point within the county. Moreover, the

* *Infra* p. 175.

commitment to urban center concentrations was not firm. The map of selected centers was apparently intended to be definitive rather than suggestive. But this decision comes through weakly, and the plan falls back on a suggestion that urban centers will probably be related to existing development. This policy may have avoided some of the hard difficulties of advance planning in uncommitted areas, but it did so at the cost of relegating the undeveloped areas to the continuance of their present status for the duration of the plan. Add to this circumstance the fact that the plan had no policy on the size, character, rate and priority of development of the urban centers that were tentatively selected, and we can conclude that the zoning authorities were left without effective guidelines. In short, nothing in the comprehensive plan firmly told the zoning agencies which were the preferred locations for apartment development. Whether a tighter and firmer set of priorities would have been either workable or desirable is entirely another matter.

We then saw that the policies of the plan tended to break down even more as they came to be applied in the zoning process. Initial distinctions between high density and lower-density apartment development were all but dropped. Proximity to arterials turned out not to be as determinative of zoning success as the plan had indicated, for the planners at least required proximity to business development as an additional necessary condition. With this qualification to the apartment zoning criteria in mind, we looked next at the relationship between adjacent uses and the apartment zoning result. We noted that the zoning agencies were reasonably faithful to the plan, at least insofar as the balance of approvals in cases of adjacent business development was favorable. But we noted that the planning commission and the board were more favorable to apartment development than the planners in cases in which the area surrounding the proposed apartment rezone was comparatively undeveloped, an attitude which we had to characterize as contrary to the plan's intentions.

But the most unexpected and at the same time most difficult problem was presented by the presence of a large number of zoned but unbuilt apartment and business areas adjacent to the apartment zoning sites which appeared in our sample. Both the commission and the board were more willing than the plan-

ners to grant new apartment zonings in areas in which the surrounding development was low intensity, but in which some
high intensity unused zoning was present. How to evaluate this
record is a difficult matter. From one perspective, of course, the
planners were simply being faithful to the plan in resisting what
some observers would call speculation. Giving effect to undeveloped rezones in later cases tends to shift initiative to the private
sector, as it impedes the ability of the zoning agencies to use
existing but undeveloped zoning as a control over the development process. Moreover, the urban centers concept of the plan
is arguably weakened by overcommitting possibly strategic areas
of the county in advance of actual development. From another
point of view, of course, a willingness to credit future development intentions is better planning to the extent that it is based
on future rather than existing development patterns. A more
mundane influence which might explain the more favorable reaction of the commission and board to apartment rezones in
undeveloped areas is the absence of a developed residential environment which allegedly would be harmed by the apartment
intrusion. At the most, in many of these cases, existing single
family development was scattered. We noted earlier that the
harm-oriented posture of the nuisance cases weakened the impact of nuisance lawsuits in areas in which the land use pattern
was not fixed. Now we see that these very same limitations may
weaken the impact of the zoning ordinance in undeveloped areas as well, especially when adjacent business and apartment zoning suggests that the surrounding area will be developed compat-
ibly with the new apartment zoning that is under consideration.

There is yet another side to this problem. We noted in an
earlier chapter that we would have expected that developer behavior would be heavily influenced by the degree of uncertainty
that exists in the local zoning process. In King County, not even
the board of county commissioners was all that favorable to
developers, and this fact plus a tendency to make ad hoc decisions on zoning applications may well have encouraged the
holding of rezoned sites. From this perspective, the banking of
rezonings for future use can be characterized as a justifiable
hedge against risk under conditions of some uncertainty.

This tendency to hold back rezoned areas from development would have been encouraged by another element in the

King County picture which has not yet been mentioned, but which could have been expected to weigh heavily with private developers. Local boundary adjustment commissions had been authorized by the Washington state legislature just prior to the period of this study, and the local boundary agency in King County appeared to have adopted a policy of federalizing the county by encouraging both new incorporations and annexations by existing municipalities. Bellevue, a large middle class suburb in the corridor between the two lakes, had embarked on a vigorous annexation policy at the time of this study. It was motivated in part by reaction against a county zoning record which was considered too favorable to apartment development. While not motivated by apartment zoning policy, a large new suburb in the southwestern area of the county was also on its way to incorporation as the study concluded. Annexations and new incorporations in the county provide yet another dimension to the risks and uncertainties inherent in the rezone process.

So far, we have been examining King County zoning policies on the basis of the planning predicates which were contained in the King County plan. These, to use Professor Dyckman's words, reflected the middle class aesthetic he found so dominant in planning thought in their emphasis on simplified activity relationships that stressed amenity and accessibility. But we have noted a wider interest in zoning and planning issues which we find unexpressed in the King County plan, and which is attentive to the impact of community planning on community objectives which lie outside the conventional concerns described by Professor Dyckman. We found an expression of this interest in what we called the "new" Equal Protection. We have already suggested, from this perspective, that local zoning and planning policy should be examined for its impact on racial and on low income housing objectives. How does King County planning and zoning fare under this approach to social accounting?

On some counts, King County apartment zoning policies had positive consequences for low income housing objectives. There was no blatant policy of exclusion, and to the extent that zoning policies emphasized convenient access to highways, they would appear functional to a housing policy for income groups who must rely heavily on public transportation. On the other hand, one important need in low income housing is for large sites at comparatively low prices, both to hold down land costs and to afford builders the cost advantages of scale economies. If this is so, then we have to conclude that the commission and board were more sensitive to this problem than the planners, for it was these agencies which reversed the recommendations of the planning department to permit more apartment rezones on larger tracts in undeveloped areas. The shift in attitude was marginal, of course, and differences in outlook are qualified by the fact that the rezone sites in our sample tended to be quite small. Even so, a tighter policy would have kept apartment rezones closer to areas of existing urbanization, would have lessened the availability of the larger tracts, and would no doubt have meant higher land prices as well. In other words, the concentration policy of the comprehensive plan would seem to run contrary to a low income housing policy which seeks to maximize the opportunities for housing development on large tracts at reasonable prices.

It is in the less developed areas favored by the commission and board, however, that we might expect less convenient accessibility to employment centers and higher journey-to-work costs that would detract from the desirability of low income housing. We cannot have it both ways unless we adopt an explicit policy of industrial decentralization, a policy which is difficult in an area with the topographical barriers and existing industrial commitments of the Seattle region. We should add, of course, that increasing accessibility by moving industrial locations to the urban periphery will also have an inflationary effect on the price of land. If cheap land is the principal objective of housing policy, then the King County planners might well have done better to adopt the development model of diffusion and dispersal, which they rejected in their comprehensive plan statement. We clearly need to sort out more rigorously just what it is we are trying to achieve in our planning for an urban environment.

This point needs to be underscored, for public intervention in the land development market carries heavy penalties for the losers and substantial gains for the winners. If zoning is not to result in arbitrary decision-making, it must be based on a policy which sensitively discriminates between cases of refusal and cases of approval on grounds which are supportable in matters of substance and of equity. None of the variables which were isolated for study—and which the plan selected—in the King County rezoning process had an appreciably high explanatory value. Both the plan and the King County zoning agencies were caught between a desire to handle what they saw as land use externalities, and a desire to implement a plan for the future of the physical environment, however imperfectly that plan might have been articulated. A zoning process caught in ambiguities such as these cannot succeed. If the King County zoning study teaches anything, it teaches the need for a reexamination of the postulates of our planning and zoning process, and of the legal framework which we employ to carry it out. We turn to this task in our final chapter.

# CHAPTER 4 APPENDIX A
## EFFECT OF DEGREE OF DENSITY CHANGE
## ON ZONING RESULT

In almost all of the cases in the study sample the rezone site was originally zoned for a low density, single family use, and an apartment use at much higher residential densities was requested. By comparing the density of the existing zone on the site with the density of the apartment zone that was requested, it is possible to determine the degree of density change in each of the apartment rezone cases. This information was in turn entered on the data cards and the computer was asked to compare the degree of density change with the zoning results. This tabulation is presented in Appendix Table 1.

An analysis of this table indicates that degree of density change did not have a significant impact on the zoning decision. We would have expected that the degree of density change would have been highest in the undeveloped areas of the county. Some indication that this is so is provided by the fact that the average size of the rezone sites when the density change was the most was around 12 acres. In all other categories the average size of the rezone site was around three acres. Even so, differences in the degree of density change do not appear to have a significant influence on the rezone result.

Appendix Table 2 compares the degree of density change with the zoning adjacent to the apartment rezone site. We should especially notice the large number of adjacent apartment zones in cases in which the degree of density change was the least, suggesting that in these cases the zoning pattern was relatively intense. Even so, the record in these cases is not noticeably that favorable, perhaps reflecting the resistance to extending apartment development in some areas. These results might be explained by the failure of apartment developers to take advantage of the higher densities even when they were approved. Comparative indifference to degree of density change on the part of the zoning agencies may have reflected this failure.

169

## APPENDIX TABLE 1. EFFECT OF DEGREE OF DENSITY CHANGE ON ZONING RESULT

| DEGREE OF DENSITY CHANGE | PLANNING DEPARTMENT | | PLANNING COMMISSION | | BOARD OF COMMISSIONERS | |
|---|---|---|---|---|---|---|
| | APPROVE | DENY | APPROVE | DENY | APPROVE | DENY |
| MOST[1] | 30 | 45 | 35 | 40 | 8 | 8 |
| MODERATE[2] | 22 | 20 | 22 | 20 | 9 | 4 |
| LEAST[3] | 24 | 26 | 26 | 24 | 5 | 5 |

[1] In these cases the original zoning was one dwelling unit to the acre or less.

[2] In these cases the degree of density change was from 36 to 44 dwelling units to the acre.

[3] In these cases the degree of density change was from 12 to 21 dwelling units to the acre.

## APPENDIX TABLE 2. RELATIONSHIP BETWEEN DEGREE OF DENSITY CHANGE AND ADJACENT ZONING

ADJACENT
ZONING:

| | MOST | MODERATE | LEAST |
|---|---|---|---|
| APARTMENT | 20 | 14 | 32 |
| BUSINESS | 25 | 14 | 6 |
| LOW DENSITY RESIDENTIAL | 22 | 14 | 10 |
| DEGREE OF DENSITY CHANGE | MOST | MODERATE | LEAST |

## CHAPTER 4 APPENDIX B

## CHI SQUARE ANALYSIS OF INFLUENCE OF ADJACENT USE AND ADJACENT ZONING ON ZONING RESULT

The results of the Chi Square analysis were as follows:

| SIGNIFICANCE OF ADJACENT USE IN RECORD OF: | P LESS THAN: |
|---|---|
| PLANNING DEPARTMENT | 0.00001 |
| PLANNING COMMISSION | 0.00138 |
| BOARD OF COUNTY COMMISSIONERS | 0.75789 |
| FINAL OUTCOME | 0.00238 |

| SIGNIFICANCE OF ADJACENT ZONING IN RECORD OF: | P LESS THAN: |
|---|---|
| PLANNING DEPARTMENT | 0.00150 |
| PLANNING COMMISSION | 0.00044 |
| BOARD OF COUNTY COMMISSIONERS | 0.58221 |
| FINAL OUTCOME | 0.00016 |

We might advance an explanation for the inconclusive results in the board of county commissioner's record. One possibility, of course, is that there simply were not enough cases appealed to the board to produce a sufficiently characteristic sample of the zoning caseload. Otherwise, we might conclude that factors other than the plan criteria were influencing the board's action. This hypothesis is somewhat negated by the failure of the board to respond negatively in cases where there had been public opposition to the zone change.

An analysis of the board's record may provide a more helpful clue. Of the 43 cases appealed to the board, the planning department and planning commission had concurred in the result in all but seven. We noted earlier an informal policy on the part of the board not to change the result in these cases. Indeed, we find that in only five of the cases was there board reversal of a joint concurrence by department and commission. Practically all of these cases, as the planners suggested, occurred late in the study period. What we find, then, is a favorable presumption applied to a decision below that achieved joint concurrence, and it would seem that it was this presumption which kept the adjacent use and zoning categories from having a statistical significance in the board's decisions. There is a striking analogue to the presumption of constitutionality applied in judicial opinions, which is used by the courts to avoid facing the policy issues in zoning controversies!

# Chapter 5

# ROLE AND PURPOSE IN THE
# PLANNING AND ZONING PROCESS

We can now conclude with some final comments on the role we see for the exercise of planning and zoning powers, and on the legal framework which will be needed to make this role effective. We can begin with the observation that we have discovered, even in the exercise of the traditional zoning function, a complex system in which many variables interact which are difficult for the legal system to control. Not all of these variables have been fully incorporated in the legal structure, and some that are have been handled indifferently. The problem springs from the regulatory dilemma which the zoning ordinance must face, and which we have described. Zoning had its origins in nuisance law, and was at first limited to the adjustment of land use incompatibilities and the prevention of harmful land use externalities at the neighborhood scale. But zoning, especially as it implements the planning process, has moved beyond mere externality prevention. We attempted our own rationale for this expansion of the planning and zoning power by suggesting that a community—municipality, county, region—might internalize at the community level the spillovers that nuisance law saw as external to the individual lot owner when it dealt with litigation between disagreeing neighbors. From its perspective, the community can allocate externalities, both negative and positive, under a set of internal values that reflect the community interest, as it is expressed in the comprehensive plan. But the shift to the community level as the basis for plan-making and policy-making carries difficulties in decision-making which do not arise in the more limited, nuisance-oriented, zoning context. While nuisance litigation and the limited kind of zoning ordinance which followed it were concerned solely with preventing harmful externalities from occurring in the private development process, leaving the private entrepre-

175

neur substantially unregulated except as he affects others, a comprehensive plan like the one we found in King County makes development allocations which go far beyond externality control.

In the wake of a plan like this we find serious problems of equity, for the plan made development choices which are supportable only at the county level, and which may make no sense at all in the narrower, neighborhood context in which the more conventional zoning controls are tested. Apartment developers who are refused zoning under the plan's policies can argue that they have been unfairly treated when other developers have been given apartment zoning at comparable locations. Justification for the difference in treatment must come directly from the policies of the plan.

We have considered the judicial response to the equity problem, and while the cases that consider these problems in the context of a comprehensive plan are still few, we noted judicial reluctance to approve differential treatment of similar locations in the name of a comprehensive plan. We have examined the King County experience to see with what success their comprehensive plan was applied in the zoning process, and here we found that the policies of the King County plan were not sufficiently clear to guide the zoning authorities. The plan failed to make explicit the restrictions on choice which are inherent in any policy whose land use allocations require different treatments of substantially identical locations. The plan compromised the policy extremes, at least to the extent that it compared these extremes on a concentration-dispersal axis. Having selected a compromise that called for centers of urban concentration, the decision on where these centers should be located was not made firm.

We want to examine more closely the reasons why these compromises in plan-making occur, and what effect they have on the implementation of the comprehensive planning process through zoning. Here we will note those problems of plan implementation which in practice make inevitable the compromises we discovered in King County. Some of these problems have been discussed earlier, and perhaps the most important point to make is that public agencies probably do not control enough of the inputs into the land development process to make the public control of land use and land development fully effective. Planning and zoning agencies may make land use and development allocations, but as the initiative for development remains in the private sector they have no control over the pace and location of development that occurs in response to planning and zoning proposals. Limited and restrictive allocations of areas in which development is allowed can provide one way out of this difficulty, but we suggested that restrictive regulation of this type will simply encourage long-term land holding at the strategic points which the plan selects. Providing location alternatives is one way to avoid this problem, but a looser planning framework carries its own penalties as long as the planning agency and the zoning authority cannot control the pace of entry into the development process, and cannot effectively control the development choices that the private market makes.

Size of development sites is another important factor, and introduces its own complications. Apartment rezone sites in the King County study were small, and were difficult to handle under the plan's policy assumptions. We do not mean to say that a policy for the absorption of small sites into the development process is impossible. But we do say that such factors as the level of outstanding rezones in relationship to the pace of development, and the responsiveness of developers to planning objectives in strategic areas, are fit matters for consideration in the planning and zoning process. For example, the zoning authority may well decide to cancel outstanding rezones in an area in which development does not follow in a reasonable time, if developer interest in another area is more pronounced, and if development in either place is consistent with the plan although development in both would compromise the planning policy. Courts would have to be convinced that the fine tuning of zoning controls to the demands of the private market is a proper public objective. We saw steps in this direction in King County. But they were tentative, and the tendency of King County planners to restrict apartment development in the name of oversupply sounds like protectionism, whatever its benign origins.

These problems of implementation are not helped appreciably by greater use of the planned development technique in zoning administration, which we described earlier. Planned unit development regulations have a variety of objectives, but they function in large part as a technique which improves site design, enhances amenities, and protects against harmful externalities by requiring a comprehensive review of an entire development as a single entity. Standing alone, planned unit development can do nothing about the problems of planning implementation which we have been discussing.

To the extent that the planned development method forces larger tracts into the zoning process, of course, the chances for implementing the objectives of the comprehensive plan through any one development proposal are increased. We saw an example of this possibility in the *Bigenho* case. We might take an additional step, which has occasionally been recommended, and either require all development in urbanizing areas to occur on large tracts or provide substantial incentives for large-scale development when it does occur. But I even doubt that forcing development along these lines will be enough.

We will probably have to take more drastic measures to overcome the obstacles to plan implementation I have described, and I have suggested that we may have to abandon entirely a land use control system which leaves the legal right to the use of land in private ownership. One possibility is to socialize the development value of land in undeveloped areas, [185] transferring this value to the public and leaving the private sector only the profit-making possibilities that lie in construction and development. Whether so drastic a change in the allocation of public and private interest would leave enough incentive to attract the private entrepreneur is another question. We may find it necessary to confer substantial entrepreneurial powers on the public sector as well, by authorizing compulsory acquisition in undeveloped areas to assemble enough land for development at the right places, in accordance with the comprehensive plan's proposals. Conferring these powers on public agencies may be both necessary and desirable, and I have recommended it. But so radical a step requires careful thought to its implications. One effect of this revision in the land use and development system is to change drastically the conditions under which gains and losses are distributed by the planning process. We will turn to a discussion of this problem later, but this proposal raises

---

[185] *See* Mandelker, *New Incentives and Controls*, in Environment and Policy 389, 403 (W.R. Ewald ed. 1968).

other, more difficult, issues. We have noted that the plan must
be sure of its policies if it is to be used to compel zoning
decisions which require that one developer be treated differently from another in similar circumstances. We then noted the
difficulties in plan implementation that make it difficult to apply policies consistently, and we turned to a consideration of
changes in the plan implementation process which would
strengthen it. Now we must pause. Weaknesses in the plan implementation machinery have led us to propose radical corrective measures, but I would suggest that we cannot propose improvement of the legal system for planning and zoning without
first questioning the values which planning has asked the legal
system to implement. The policies selected in the planning process determine the nature of the plan, and influence the character of the legal techniques that must be used to carry it out.
Moreover, we will suggest that not only our question of fairness
in plan implementation, but the more conventional problems
raised by uncompensated regulation, are deeply affected by the
choices made in the planning process. Let us see why this is so.

### Planning Goals and Planning Choice

This discussion takes us directly to an examination of the
substantive content of the comprehensive plan which is produced in the planning process. We can generalize our discussion
of content by returning once more to our urban limits illustra-
tion, and to a discussion of the urban aesthetic which appears to
be implicit in the typical planning response to the urban limits
problem. We noted earlier that American planning practice had
not been overly concerned with the urban limits question. While
this observation may be correct as a general observation, American planning agencies at the regional level have at least considered the problem of containing urban growth. Their policies on
containment, moreover, reflect an urban aesthetic which places
a high value on concentration, and on the need for clean distinctions between the concentrated and less concentrated segments of metropolitan areas. It is true, of course, that some
concentration would occur even without a plan, but plans like
the King County plan urge concentration levels at selected

points which go beyond what the market would produce, undirected.

In our King County example we did not have, strictly speaking, a regional planning agency, but we did have a county which was at least large enough to embrace a substantial part of a region. If we take the King County plan as a typical regional plan for purposes of evaluating regional planning efforts, sophisticated planners might urge that we have done better since. I am not sure. But let us pursue our inquiry into the choices implicit in a planning policy on containment by looking more closely at what has happened to regional planning in the Washington, D.C., metropolitan area. Regional planning in this area is certainly as advanced as it is anywhere in the country.

Remember that in 1964, the year the King County plan appeared, a regional plan was prepared for the Washington, D.C., metropolitan area which provided the planning backdrop for our discussion of the Maryland apartment cases. Remember also that the Washington regional plan called for the development of the Washington region in a radial pattern of wedges and corridors. This plan is still official policy in the Washington area, whatever the difficulties it has presented in implementation, and the Maryland-National Capital Park and Planning Commission has just issued as of this writing the latest of its area plans which are seen as implementary of the wedges and corridors concept—a preliminary master plan for the Bowie-Collington area in outer Prince Georges County. [186] I think it is correct to say that the Bowie-Collington plan is a fair example of the current state-of-the-art in regional land use planning.

We are struck, therefore, as we look at the Bowie-Collington plan, with its resemblance to the King County effort which appeared some six years earlier. Like the King County plan, the Bowie-Collington plan predicates its proposal on the broadest kinds of planning objectives ("To improve the . . . quality . . . of the area")[187] to which all would assent. There is an expression of interest in building a community to serve all income and

---

[186] Maryland-National Capital Park and Planning Comm'n, A Preliminary Master Plan for Bowie-Collington and Vicinity Planning Areas 71 and 74 (December 1969) [hereinafter cited as Plan].

[187] Plan at 3.

social (racial?) groups, but we note immediately that the residents of the area are comparatively young, well-educated, and affluent, much as in King County.

While the Bowie-Collington plan does not explicitly make the compromise between centralization and dispersion that we found in King County, the plan reaches the same objective by calling for development of a high density "new town" center, reservation of a large area to be developed at very low densities, and "suburban" densities from 1.6 to 3.0 dwelling units per acre elsewhere. How development at these densities is compatible with the objective of serving all income groups is open to question, but let us put this question aside for the moment. There is much else that can be said about the Bowie-Collington plan, but what interests us is the plan's provision for apartments. Here we learn that "urban" (apartment?) densities are to be limited to new town and major community centers. But note:

> This does not preclude the provision of multi-family housing facilities in the suburban communities under circumstances where, by means of proper site design and the provision of required open spaces, such development could be accommodated within the framework of the gross suburban density objectives recommended by the plan.[188]

In other words, the Maryland planners are not willing, as the planners were in King County, to allow apartment development to increase density levels except in a limited number of high intensity development centers. Just how much apartment development this policy really contemplates we are not told, but it is clear that if apartment development may not raise density levels in the "suburban" areas then the incentive for such development in these sections has largely been withdrawn. We might note, incidentally, that the Bowie-Collington plan proposes three alternate though geographically close sites for their proposed new town, where apartment development is to be encouraged.

---

[188] Plan at 4.

We digress to present the Bowie-Collington plan in this much detail only to reinforce our observation that regional planning of the typical American variety prefers a development strategy in which the extremes between high intensity and low intensity development are pronounced,[189] and in which the limitations on development opportunities at concentrated levels requires powerful and restrictive plan implementation techniques if the policies of the plan are to be carried out. We might now ask what consequences there are in this kind of planning to which the legal system should give attention? We could argue, of course, that the selection of an appropriate urban form is beyond the legal venue, and that Americans can live in corridors, clusters, or new town centers, if that is what they want. But let us see.

### The Legal Response to Planning Policy

Let us start with the problems of social and economic mix to which the Bowie-Collington plan said it had given attention. We should notice at once that the densities which the plan recommends for its suburban areas are very low, too low to support the multi-family or high density development which seems essential if housing is to be built to serve low income groups. Higher "urban" densities are to be provided in the new town, but if so then I think we will find low income and racial minorities concentrated in the new town, while well-educated, affluent, whites continue to populate the suburban sections. In other words, the plan will carry the racial and economic separation so characteristic of our older urban areas to the newer suburbs. Whether we want this kind of racial and economic cleavage is a good question, and our analysis suggests a basis on which alert "third party" minorities can assert a constitutional interest in planning and zoning questions. The segregation problem arises as much from the physical model of development

---

[189] *See* the discussion of regional transportation planning in D.E. Boyce & N.D. Day, Metropolitan Plan Evaluation Methodology (1969). *See also* the review of planning theory literature in Hightower, *Planning Theory in Contemporary Professional Education*, 35 J. Am. Institute of Planners 326 (1969).

which the plan projects as it does from more blatant exclusion through very low density zoning, which has been singled out as the main villain.

Let us now turn to some of the more traditional legal issues in zoning and planning. If anything, Bowie-Collington calls for a more concentrated pattern than the King County plan. While the King County plan selected several points for high density development, Bowie-Collington calls for a concentration of density in a new town at only one point in the planning area. Much of the difference in objective is due to the fact that the Bowie-Collington plan covers a much smaller area—only 60 square miles—but even so the new town center, planned for 200 to 400 acres, is bigger than anything the King County plan contemplated. Now the fact is that a development this size creates problems of implementation much more serious than anything proposed for King County.[190] If we thought that tough decisions had to be made in King County about areas of preference for high intensity development, they are dwarfed by what will be required by a plan like Bowie-Collington. For example, the plan recommends only one regional shopping center in the Bowie-Collington area, and it is to be in the new town.[191] Nor are problems of implementation made any easier by the adoption of a "Staging District" map which creates development priorities by area.[192] If, as we have suggested, plan implementation is seriously qualified by lack of control over entry into the development process, then planning strategies with demands as stringent as these will be hard to implement. We will need more control over freedom of choice in making development decisions than we have had or than we may tolerate, and I doubt whether the traditional system is up to it without the addition of compulsory powers of acquisition and development to which I referred above.

These reflections lead us to another thought that has considerable consequence for our legal institutions, and it flows directly from the preference patterns which we see exhibited in plans

---

[190] *See* Mandelker, *A Legal Strategy for Urban Development*, in Planning for a Nation of Cities 209 (S.B. Warner ed. 1966).

[191] Plan at 11.

[192] Plan at 13.

like Bowie-Collington. Any planning proposal carries its own tradeoff between freedom of choice in development opportunity and a restriction of that opportunity in the name of a larger community objective. Given an urban aesthetic which favors a concentration policy, trading off in the community's direction means trading off in favor of greater restrictiveness on development opportunity in the area covered by the plan. We expressed this idea in our discussion of urban limit policies, and we see a restrictive policy on urban limits in a plan like Bowie-Collington, which limits narrowly the opportunities for development at an intense scale. In more concrete terms, a shopping center to serve an entire region is limited to a new town of 200 to 400 acres, the new town to be selected from three closely-placed alternative locations in an area of some 60 square miles.

We saw the effect of a narrow urban limits policy of this kind in our earlier discussion. There we noted that narrowing the urban circumference in relation to demand will limit the number of available development sites, has an inflationary effect on the prices of those sites that are available, and increases the zoning competition for those sites that are permitted to enter the development process. In legal terms, a tight policy aggravates the conventional Due Process objection, for if the number of sites allocated for development is limited then the value of each of these sites will be higher than if more were available. As a consequence, land values will fall more steeply on those sites on which development is not to be allowed, and the disparity in value between the restricted sites and the favored sites will seem greater. The developer who seeks a zoning change will be able to show a larger "loss" in value as the basis for his claim that the zoning restriction, as applied to him, has deprived him of "property" without Due Process of Law. No doubt it is pressures such as these, explicitly recognized or not, which lead planners like those in King County to a less restrictive plan, and which encourage lay members of boards and commissions to hasten the invasion of less developed and urbanized areas. We might note, in passing, the other side of this problem. A tighter planning policy also increases the monetary gains of those developers who win. Under the present system, their gains go unrecouped by the public, as much as the losses suffered by the losers go uncompensated.

We asked earlier what role the legal system should play in judging planning and zoning policies, and we might now consider in light of our discussion just how the law might handle the losses and gains which accrue from the operation of the planning and zoning system. There are several possibilities. One is to recognize the impact of the regulatory system on the distribution of loss and gain, and to balance the impact of the system by compensating for all losses and by taxing away all gains. I have urged an approach similar to this elsewhere;[193] it has the advantage of doing equity throughout the planning and zoning jurisdiction, and there is precedent for it in the English system, which taxes away *some* of the gain and which compensates *some* of the losses.[194] But the English have the advantage that they can make these wealth distributions on the national level. In the United States, these determinations would be left to local government units under our present governmental arrangements. The temptation to favoritism may be too much to endure, not to mention the fact that wealth distribution measures of this sort may do more harm than good unless carried out in a market sufficiently large to include all of the area in which the effect of planning and zoning judgments is felt. I doubt that we are ready to take this step in this country.

We would also want to make exceptions to full compensation for loss in value from zoning restrictions. The very basis of zoning regulation in externality protection argues against compensation for the landowner who is merely being asked to absorb external costs which have properly been assigned to him, and which the private market cannot assess. But this suggestion runs counter to our conclusion that even the identification of "harmful" externalities requires value choices. We may have to limit our exception to developed areas, and to intrusions on which there is a high consensus about detrimental effect. Dirty industry in residential areas provides one example. Here the nuisance tradition is helpful, and judicial nonrecognition of loss in these cases can properly be carried forward into our land use regulation scheme. But this solution is more pragmatic than it is consistent.

---

[193] Mandelker, *supra* note 185, at 401-03.

[194] For discussion see Mandelker, *Notes from the English: Compensation in Town and Country Planning*, 49 Calif. L. Rev. 699, 736-41 (1961).

There are even deeper objections to full taxation of gain, many of which are familiar. One is that the linkage between public development policies and capital appreciation in land value is not all that clear. Capital appreciation in land merely reflects the increasingly intense pressure for the use of land that comes with urbanization, so that planning and zoning policies affect the distribution of that gain more than its creation. In recognition of this fact, the English only provide for partial capture of increment in development value which flows from planning and zoning decisions.[195] We might add that the earlier English experience with full taxation of gain broke down in part for another reason. To the extent that expectation of capital appreciation attracts investor interest in the land market, full taxation of all gain removes any reason for that interest. So long as the ownership of land remains in private hands, we must provide some incentive for land investment and land holding if that market is to operate at all.

We might now return to our earlier observation that the magnitude of gain and loss which accrues from the planning and zoning system simply reflects the restrictiveness with which the planning policy is applied.[196] Under a restrictive and concentrated planning policy, like Bowie-Collington for example, losses in capital appreciation will seem greater just because the range in the intensity of permitted development is greater between the high-intensity and low-intensity development sectors. We would now urge that the legal system should be more concerned with the tradeoff that occurs between restrictiveness and freedom in development than with the more traditional and contrived problem of loss in development value from zoning restrictions. How to express this concern is another matter. One possibility is to provide for public acquisition of those areas in which high-intensity development is permitted, on the grounds that this is the best way to recapture for the public the gain in value that development at these densities brings. Outside these areas, we would apply the compensation formula we have outlined above, exempting only those losses which we can identify

---

[195] *Id.*

[196] Mandelker, *The Role of Law in the Planning Process*, 30 Law & Contemp. Prob. 26, 33 (1965).

as a proper absorption of harmful externalities.[197] Let us now observe that this approach to the implementation of the comprehensive plan dissolves the fairness-equity issue, if we argue that compensation has been afforded to the landowner in all those cases in which the regulatory burden placed on him is judged to be insupportable. But this method of plan implementation does not dissolve the fairness-equity issue if we see it as more than a question of compensated and uncompensated burden, and regard it primarily as a question of choice-making among a cluster of alternatives. Landowners who are compensated for losses in value that come from being placed in a restricted zone may still want to argue the basis for their selection, and may contend with fervor that they and not someone else should have been marked for acquisition in the high-density development area. Problems of choice, in other words, do not go away simply because the consequence of that choice is different. We had noted this point much earlier in our discussion of the landowner's possible objection to having his land taken for a highway, even though he is fully compensated.

If we find that choices are always required no matter what the compensatory base for the planning and zoning system, then we will always have with us the problems of equity which Reich has brought to our attention. Choice-making and allocation in the land planning process must then fall back on the values which that process has decided to maximize. Moreover, if we feel that there are legal grounds for examining that choice, and our discussion has suggested that there are, then we would have to include in our legal system the opportunity for appraising the planning judgment. It is the choices that are made in the planning process, and the distribution of gains and losses which they confer, that create the problem. Review of this kind is arguably beyond the judicial competence, however bold the language of the dissenting judge might have been in the *Vickers*

---

[197] *See* Mandelker, *Controlling Land Values in Areas of Rapid Urban Expansion*, 12 U.C.L.A.L. Rev. 707, 734 (1965). As the article indicates, even this approach is not without its difficulties in practice. Moreover, we must distinguish between the compensable event and the amount of compensation payable. Our earlier discussion of the nature of the constitutional claim for loss of development value suggests that we would want to place some limits on the amount of compensation recoverable. For discussion of the English solution to these problems see Mandelker, *supra* note 194.

opinion, which we quoted in the first chapter. And I doubt whether we have the political will to create the legislative and administrative structure to carry out the kind of appraisal I have in mind.

We do not even wish to ask, in the context of our discussion, whether the balance between restrictiveness and freedom which is struck by the King County plan and plans like Bowie-Collington is acceptable, or even whether it is necessary to a planning strategy for our urban areas. What we want to stress is that these are the kinds of questions we must begin to ask if we are even to begin to understand the value predicates on which our planning and urban policies are based. In the absence of thoroughgoing attention to these issues, we are left with the inequities inherent in the existing system, and I would suggest that the problems will be solved as they were in King County— by compromise.

We now confront the problem of values and the manner of their implementation, with which we concluded the first chapter. We wondered whether the zoning system was as much an innocent regulator of potentially harmful activity as it seemed, and we have concluded that any zoning system which seeks real limitation on freedom of choice must carry well-delineated and value-laden policies with it. These are determined in the planning process, and expressed in the comprehensive plan. Unfortunately, we have not been as rigorous as we should in examining the impact of our planning judgments on our zoning strategies, and on the role the legal system should play in appraising, validating, and limiting both. We are simply not sure of the values we wish to implement in our urban policies. Until we are, we can continue to expect the planning and zoning process to be deeply troubled by ambiguity and ambivalence.

# BIBLIOGRAPHY

What follows is a selected listing of additional articles and books which deal with the problems raised in this book. Additional references to source material on planning can also be found in the recently issued and extremely helpful review in D.B. Holleb, *Social and Economic Information for Urban Planning* (1969), which is available from the U.S. Government Clearinghouse, Warrenton, Virginia (PB 184 006). Excellent bibliographies are also issued periodically by the Council of Planning Librarians.

### The Planning Function in Zoning
### and Land Use Control

American Institute of Planners, Planning for Social Change (1969).

Babcock, R.F., The Zoning Game: Municipal Practices and Policies (1966).

Berry, E.C., The Racial Aspects of Urban Planning (Chicago Urban League 1968).

Bettman, A., City and Regional Planning Papers (Harvard City Planning Studies 1946).

Burby, R.J., Politics and Planning: Toward a Model of Planning-Related Policy Inputs in American Local Government (1968).

Clark, R.A., Selected References on Land Use Planning, Council of Planning Librarians, Exchange Bibliography No. 92 (1969).

Dyckman, J.W., An Individual Review of Current Planning Literature, Council of Planning Librarians, Exchange Bibliography No. 36 (1967).

Fagin, H., *The Evolving Philosophy of Urban Planning*, in Urban Research and Policy Planning 309 (L.F. Schnore & H. Fagin eds. 1967).

Hagman, D., Planning and Development Control Law (1971)

Heifetz, R., An Annotated Bibliography on the Changing Scope of Urban Planning in the U.S.A., Council of Planning Librarians, Exchange Bibliography No. 86 (1969).

Kaufman, J.L., Current Trends in Planning and Their Effect on Planning Literature, Council of Planning Librarians, Exchange Bibliography No. 101 (1969).

Kent, T.J., The Urban General Plan (1964).

New York Office of Planning Coordination, Planning for Development in New York State (1970).

New Zoning, The (N. Marcus & N.W. Groves eds. 1970).

Rabinovitz, F.F., City Politics and Planning (1969).

Scott, M., American City Planning Since 1890 (1969).

Urban Planning Guide (W.H. Claire ed. 1969).

U.S. Library of Congress, Legislative Reference Service, Urban Planning: A Bibliography, 1960-68 (1968).

Willheim, S., Urban Zoning and Land Use Theory (1962).

---

Bolan, *Emerging Views of Planning*, 33 J. Am. Institute of Planners 233 (1967).

Broady, *The Social Context of Urban Planning*, 4 Urban Affairs Q. 335 (1969).

Chapin, *Taking Stock of Technique for Shaping Urban Growth*, 29 J. Am. Institute of Planners 76 (1963).

Christensen, *Land Use Control for the New Community*, 6 Harv. J. Legis. 496 (1969).

Doeble, *Horse Sense About Zoning and the Master Plan*, 13 Zoning Digest 209 (1961).

Dyckman, *Social Planning, Social Planners, and Planned Societies*, 32 J. Am. Institute of Planners 66 (1966).

Feiss, *Planning Absorbs Zoning*, 27 J. Am. Institute of Planners 121 (1961).

Frieden, *The Changing Prospects for Social Planning*, 33 J. Am. Institute of Planners 311 (1967).

Haar, *The Master Plan: An Impermanent Constitution*, 20 Law & Contemp. Prob. 351 (1955).

Hoover, *On Master Plans and Constitutions*, 26 J. Am. Institute of Planners 5 (1960).

McBride & Babcock, *The Master Plan—A Statutory Prerequisite to a Zoning Ordinance*, 12 Zoning Digest 353 (1960).

Mocine, *Urban Physical Planning and the "New Planning,"* 32 J. Am. Institute of Planners 234 (1966).

Perrin, *The Noiseless Secession from the Comprehensive Plan*, 33 J. Am. Institute of Planners 336 (1967).

Petersen, *On Some Meanings of "Planning,"* 32 J. Am. Institute of Planners 130 (1966).

Webber, *The Roles of Intelligence Systems in Urban Systems Planning*, 31 J. Am. Institute of Planners 289 (1965).

Wheaton, *Operations Research for Metropolitan Planning*, 29 J. Am. Institute of Planners 250 (1963).

Williams, *Planning Law and Democratic Living*, 20 Law & Contemp. Prob. 317 (1955).

Williams, *Planning Law and the Supreme Court: I*, 13 Zoning Digest 57 (1961).

---

Comment, *Zoning: Looking Beyond Municipal Borders,* 1965 Wash. U.L.Q. 107.

## Apartments and Suburbia

Neutze, G.M., *Property Taxation and Multiple-Family Housing in Land and Building Taxes* 115 (A.P. Becker ed. 1969).

Coming to Grips with Urban Sprawl, Nations Cities, vol. 5, at 20 (August 1967).

Anderson, *Land Classification and Rural Zoning: A Discussion*, 33 J. Farm Econ. 777 (1957).

Bailey, *Effects of Race and of Other Demographic Factors on the Value of Single-Family Houses*, 42 Land Econ. 215 (1966).

Coke & Liebman, *Political Values and Population Density Control*, 37 Land Econ. 347 (1961).

Czamanski, *A Method of Forecasting Metropolitan Growth*, 6 J. Regional Sci. 35 (1965).

Davis, *Economic Elements in Municipal Zoning Decisions*, 39 Land Econ. 375 (1963).

Gottlieb, *Influences on Value in Urban Land Markets, U.S.A.*, 6 J. Regional Sci. 1 (1965).

Kaunitz, *The Mass Suburb*, 23 J. Am. Institute of Planners 195 (1957).

Morrill, *Expansion of the Urban Fringe: A Simulation Experiment in Seattle, Washington*, 15 Regional Sci. Ass'n Papers & Proc. 185 (1965).

Powers, *Age and Space Aspects of City and Suburban Housing*, 40 Land Econ. 381 (1964).

Wolfe, *A Chronology of Land Tenure: Influences on Suburban Zoning Development Patterns*, 37 Town Planning Rev. 271 (1967).

## The "Standing" Problem in Zoning

Ayer, *The Primitive Law of Standing in Land Use Disputes: Some Notes from a Dark Continent*, 55 Iowa L. Rev. 344 (1969).

Foss, *Interested Third Parties in Zoning*, 12 U. Fla. L. Rev. 16 (1959).

Comment, *Standing to Appeal Zoning Determinations, The "Aggrieved Person" Requirement*, 64 Mich. L. Rev. 1070 (1966).

Comment, *The "Aggrieved Person" Requirement in Zoning*, 8 Wm. & Mary L. Rev. 294 (1967).

# INDEX

References are to pages

## A

Amendments in zoning, 63-66, 69, 71-75, 77-83, 86-103
in King County, 127-68
Apartments,
and growth policy, 42-44, 49-50
and highways, 86, 93-96, 102-03, 117-19, 121-24, 142-44
and holdout problem, 50-51, 93, 146, 149, 164-65
and schools, 95
and sewerage facilities, 96
and water facilities, 96
as planning problem, 116-23, 180-83
as zoning problem, 21-22, 32-36, 48, 49, 51-52, 62-63, 66-77, 84-105, 111-15, 180-82
in King County, 127-68
zoning for, in Maryland, 86-105
Archdiocese of Portland v. County of Washington, 73-74, 93-94

## B

Baker v. Montgomery County Council, 97-102
Baltimore, Md. area,
planning in, 88
Bigenho v. Montgomery County Council, 102-03, 119, 140, 178
Biske v. City of Troy, 52-53, 61
Board of Adjustment, 65-66
Boundary commission,
in King County, 165-66
Bowie-Collington Plan, 180-84, 186
Brown v. Wimpress, 102-03

## C

Change-mistake rule, 90-91, 92-93, 95, 115
Cleaver v. Board of Adjustment, 75-77, 85

Comprehensive plan,
and apartments, 116-23, 180-83
and urban centers concept, 116-17, 153, 163-64
and zoning, 57-59, 62, 63-64, 68-69, 71-77, 82-83, 84-85, 91-92, 102-05, 136-46, 157, 163-67, 175-79, 183-84, 186-87
in King County, 116-23, 176
nature of, 59-63, 69-70
Comprehensive planning,
and growth policy, 41-45, 50, 179-82
and housing, 166-67, 182-83
and planned unit development, 177-78
and racial issues, 182-83
and zoning, 3, 19-20, 21, 38-41, 53-59
in King County, 107-16
in Maryland, 86-88, 91, 180-84, 185-86
in Washington state, 109, 111, 112-13
role of, 2-4, 14-16, 18-19, 20, 38-40, 61, 69-70
Conditional uses, 65-67, 68-69, 71-72, 73-75, 77-78, 103-04, 111-12
Constitutional issues,
and growth policy, 183-88
in zoning, 5-11, 19-20, 31-35, 40-41, 46, 49-50, 71-76, 77-84, 89
redefinition of, 11-18

## D

Decision-making process, 15, 16
in zoning, 60, 61-69, 112-14
Dyckman, J. W., 69-70, 166

## E

Economic analysis,
and legal controls, 24-25, 26-27
Eminent domain, 2, 4, 6, 80

193